History Around Us

History
Around Us

Nathaniel Harris

Hamlyn
London·New York·Sydney·Toronto

Acknowledgements

Illustrations by Susan Hunter, Brian Evans, Oxford Illustrators and B. L. Kearley Ltd.

The following photographs show details of paintings which are reproduced by gracious permission of Her Majesty the Queen: 96, 112 top right, 112 bottom right, 113 top, 136 top right.

Photographs

Aerofilms Ltd. 35 bottom right; Art Gallery and Temple Newsam House, Leeds 181; Bildarchiv Foto Marburg 57 top left, 72 top left; Bodleian Library 62; British Library 72 right, 107 top; British Museum 12 bottom left, 12 bottom right, 24 right, 25 bottom left, 25 right, 38–39, 40 top left, 40 top right; BR London Midland Region 157 top right; British Tourist Authority 24 bottom left, 28 right, 35 bottom left, 40 bottom right, 47 top, 47 centre, 57 bottom left, 73 left, 73 top right, 87, 92 top left, 92 bottom left, 108 bottom right, 109 left, 118–119, 126, 156, 176, 185 top left, 185 bottom left, 185 top right, back jacket inset top; British Travel Association 93 top left; Board of Trinity College, Dublin 38 right; Central Press 147; Christie's 121; Cinema Bookshop 178; Country Life Magazine 92 right, 109 right, 157 top; Courtauld Institute of Art 108 top left; W. F. Davidson front jacket; Department of the Environment – Crown copyright 11, 56 bottom, 57 top right, 184 top right; C. M. Dixon 14, 21, 22, 25 top left; EEC 173; Fox Photos 157 bottom left; Grosvenor Gallery 154; Hamlyn Group Picture Library 31, 41, 42–43, 44, 57 bottom right, 73 bottom right, 77 top right, 108 bottom left, 132 right, 136 bottom right, 143 top, 143 bottom, 148, 166, 184 bottom left; Hamlyn Group Picture Library – Ray Gardner 84, 100; Historical Picture Service 69, 140; Irish Tourist Board 132 left; C. Johnson 27; A. F. Kersting 47 bottom, 62, 133 left, back jacket; Mansell Collection 53, 68, 101, 103, 104, 129, 141, 149 top; Museum of London 15; National Buildings Record 93 right; National Gallery 130 top; National Gallery of Ireland 88; National Museum of Antiquities of Scotland 37 bottom left, 37 bottom right; National Maritime Museum 133 right; National Portrait Gallery 60, 76 left, 76 right, 77 top left, 77 bottom left, 96 bottom left, 96 right, 97 top left, 97 bottom left, 97 top right, 97 centre right, 97 bottom right, 112 left, 136 left, 137 left, 137 right; Hugh Newbury 184 bottom right; Northern Ireland Tourist Board 72 bottom left; Popperfoto 164, 172; Press Association 161 right; Rex Features 160 left, 161 left; Sanderson 153; Scala 28; Science Museum, London 113 bottom left, 116–117, 128, 152 left; Scottish Tourist Board 56 top; Shell Centre 165; Sir John Soane Museum 130 bottom; Sunday Times 160 top; Tate Gallery 55; Tate Gallery – Hamlyn Group 102, 107; Tin Research Institute 139 right; Twentieth Century Fox Film Co. Ltd. 155; Unilever 142; University of York 180; Victoria and Albert Museum – Crown copyright 70, 83, 89, 93 bottom left, back jacket inset bottom; Wallace Collection 67, 77 bottom left; Watts Gallery 139 left; Josiah Wedgwood & Sons Ltd. 117; Welwyn Hatfield District Council 166–167; Reece Winston 24 top left; Yale University Library 160 bottom; Z.E.F.A. front jacket inset. Milk Marketing Board, for reference material 163.

Published 1979 by The Hamlyn Publishing Group Limited
London · New York · Sydney · Toronto
Astronaut House, Feltham, Middlesex, England
© Copyright The Hamlyn Publishing Group Limited 1979

ISBN 0 600 39529 4   Printed by New Interlitho, Italy

Contents

Ha 455,203⁴
J942
40604
£2.75

The Prehistoric Past

History deals with times and places for which there are written records. Where these never existed, or have disappeared, we can only find out what happened from the evidence of things – from bones, tools and similar objects. This is the special job of the archaeologist. There are thousands of prehistoric sites all over the British Isles, though here we have space to mention only a few of the most famous and interesting.

Men appeared in Britain at least a quarter of a million years ago, between long periods when the land was covered with glaciers. The last of the great ice ages ended only around 9000 BC. Britain was part of the European continent until about 6000 BC, when the melting ice-caps raised the sea level and created the English and Irish Channels.

In spite of the sea barrier, a new people arrived around 4000 BC. They were more advanced than the older inhabitants, who were hunters: they were farmers, and kept sheep and cattle, though they still used stone for their tools. The age of the farmers is often called the Neolithic (New Stone) Age; the long earlier age of hunters is the Palaeolithic (Old Stone) Age.

The farmers were prudent men who dug pits in the ground to store grain. They set up camps surrounded by banks and ditches, with just

a causeway allowing entry. These 'causeway camps' provided a basic pattern for many later settlements.

The tombs built during this period were even more impressive, for death seems to have obsessed early man. The earliest of these tombs are the long barrows – huge mounds of earth, very wide at one end and tapering to a narrow tail. They were eventually provided with a stone chamber for the dead, and a courtyard at the tomb entrance. An admired example is Wayland's Smithy, on the borders of Oxfordshire and Wiltshire. At its grandest, this kind of tomb became a huge circular mound with a chamber inside, approached by a long passage lined with decorated stones. There are magnificent examples in Ireland, at New Grange, Knowth and Dowth.

All building of this kind, using great stone slabs, is called megalithic, which literally means 'great stone'. The 'lith' comes from *lithos*, the Greek word for a stone, and occurs in 'Palaeolithic' and 'Neolithic' as well.

Such grand tombs must have been built for chiefs, or perhaps high priests. This must also be true of Maes Howe in the Orkneys – a 7·5 metre mound covering a central chamber with two side vaults. The interior is constructed of stone slabs fitted together without mortar.

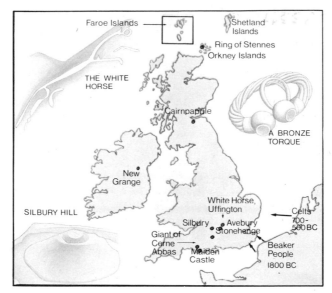

Britain before Roman Times

The dead were also cremated. The ashes might be buried in another kind of megalithic site, the henge. In its basic form this was a larger version of the causeway camp: the enclosure with bank and ditch. At first, wood rather than stone seems to have been used in henges, but use of stone speeded up with the arrival of a new people from the Continent – the Beaker People, so called because of their distinctive pottery beakers.

The most famous of the henges is of course Stonehenge in Wiltshire. The stones date from around 1800 BC, though the henge itself is earlier. The single uprights are bluestones, brought all the way from the Preseli Mountains in South Wales, probably by raft along the coast. The grey, pitted 'sarsens' must have been even harder to move. These sandstone pillars, with a bar (lintel) mortared across the top of each pair, are immensely heavy and yet must have come from the hills 32 kilometres to the north of Salisbury Plain. Tremendous labour and organisation must have gone into creating Stonehenge, and this has led to a belief that it was a great religious centre or even an astronomical observatory. Among other henges worth visiting are those at Avebury in Wiltshire, Arbor Low, Derbyshire, Cairnpapple, West Lothian, and the Ring of Stenness, Orkney.

The Beaker People introduced

7

the use of metals – copper, bronze and probably gold. So now Britain moved from the Stone Age to the Bronze Age. One result of this revolution was to make the many stone axe 'factories' obsolete. Some of these had been worked before 3000 BC, and trade and travel carried their products hundreds of kilometres. One such 'factory' was Langdale Pike in the Lake District, where flakes from the workings still litter the site.

The Beaker People seem to have shared Britain with the earlier inhabitants, identified by their 'grooved' pottery. These people lived on separately at, for example, Skara Brae on Orkney, where they built a remarkable little group of solidly-made stone houses in about 2000 BC.

From about 1200 BC a large number of defensive positions were constructed on hilltops. They are usually called hill forts, and were made by the well-tried technique of banking and ditching, creating an easily defended area big enough to hold several hundred people with their cattle. A famous hill fort, occupied down to Roman times, is Maiden Castle near Dorchester in Dorset.

Even more warlike invaders entered Britain in 650 BC. These were the Celts, who also occupied most of northern and central Europe. According to Roman writers, Celts were tall, fair and ferocious. Their language is known,

but their religion remains rather obscure. They had few temples but worshipped in sacred groves in the forests. The ceremonies conducted by their priests, the druids, seem to have involved human sacrifice, and head-hunting played a part in Celtic warfare. The Celts were also artists in metalwork, which they embellished with patterns that were crowded and complicated but very beautiful. This style survived the centuries to become part of the medieval British tradition in art.

The Celts brought with them iron tools and weapons, and ironworking techniques. The materials used for tools and weapons have played a decisive part in man's history – which is why prehistory is still divided into Stone, Bronze and Iron Ages. Iron was found in many parts of Britain, but because of primitive mining techniques it remained precious – so precious that iron bars were used as currency.

The last prehistoric conquerors were the Belgae – Celts from what are now northern France and Belgium. About 150 BC they invaded and settled south-east England. The Belgic tribes seem to have been constantly at war, and they introduced a new kind of defensive site. The *oppida* were very large areas of land in which there was room for wooden buildings, farming and cattle raising. They were surrounded by huge dykes that might be as much as 12 metres deep. These were permanent settlements, and might be considered towns.

By the first century AD, the Celts had their own coins, issued by mints set up in *oppida* and inscribed with Celtic names. Contact with Rome was frequent, especially after Caesar's conquest of Gaul (France). And luxury products such as wine and glassware found their way into the huts of the Celtic chiefs, who traded them with the Romans for slaves and corn.

Contact with powerful empires can be dangerous, as the Belgae found out when Caesar forced them to recognise Roman overlordship. The terms were vague, but they later gave the Romans an excuse to invade and conquer Britain. With the Roman occupation, the pre-history of most of Britain comes to an end.

Scotland and Ireland were not conquered, and in a sense remained prehistoric for centuries more. Life remained primitive, and much ingenuity was expended on defences. For example, artificial islands called *crannogs* were used in both countries down to the ninth century, and later still in Ireland. They were made by heaping up peat and stones and building a house on a platform. Often there was a concealed causeway to the shore, running just below the surface of the water. In Scotland there are many surviving *duns* (pronounced 'doons'), which are fortified houses of various kinds. Perhaps the most interesting of all

are the *brochs* in the west and far north of Scotland, for example Mousa, on Shetland, and Dun Carloway (another dun!) on Lewis. These are circular, thick-walled defensive towers, some rising originally more than 12 metres. In many ways they compare with later structures such as castle keeps and peel towers.

Some kinds of prehistory remain 'present' and alive. The ancient paths, for example, go on being used. Prehistoric man travelled along the ridgeways – chalk and limestone ridges rising clear of the woodlands and vegetation that covered most of the country. Such a route was the Icknield Way, running since time immemorial from the Wash in the east to Wiltshire in the south-west.

Hill figures are still more dramatic. These huge shapes, cut in chalk, were made by clearing away grass and earth on a hillside. Two survive from prehistoric times: the White Horse of Uffington, in Berkshire, and the Giant of Cerne Abbas in Dorset. Prehistoric man started a tradition with the hill figure. People have not only maintained the prehistoric figures over the centuries – they have made their own hill figures, from Anglo-Saxon times right down to the nineteenth century.

In these small but important ways, there is history in many of the things around us.

Roman Britain

The first British experience of Roman strength came in 55–54 BC, when Julius Caesar mounted two expeditions across the Channel. These were not much more than forays and were not followed up.

Almost ninety years later the Romans began a full-scale invasion, and quickly subdued the area we now call England and Wales. Despite some successes, they failed to hold down Caledonia (modern Scotland), and they never tried to cross over to Ireland.

Roman Britain lasted over 360 years. In this time wealthy Britons and people who lived in towns learned to dress and behave like Romans. For them, at least, life must have seemed much more pleasant under imperial rule. Many of their comforts and conveniences

Left: As part of the Roman empire the British learned of luxuries they had never imagined – luxuries that might be enjoyed only by the upper classes. *Above:* Pewter, glass and pottery vessels dating from the second and third centuries AD (BRITISH MUSEUM)

(central heating, baths, well-made roads) were lost when Roman Britain fell – and were not seen again for hundreds of years.

In the fourth century, 'barbarian' pressures on Roman Britain built up. Picts raided across the border from Caledonia, Scots made forays across the sea from Ireland and savage Saxon pirates came all the way from north Germany to prey on the coasts. Roman governors tried hard to cope, though they were weakened by the fact that the Mediterranean heartlands of the empire were also threatened by barbarians.

The end came all the sooner be- cause ambitious Roman generals, stationed in Britain, several times tried to seize power in the empire. When such generals marched away, they took with them the troops who were supposed to defend Britain. The last Roman soldiers seem to have left in AD 407. Three years later, the British sent a message to the emperor Honorius asking him to send troops. The emperor himself was struggling desperately for sur- vival, and told them they would have to look after themselves. This they did. Split into rival kingdoms, the Romanised British still managed to carry on for over a century after the legions left. But gradually they yielded to the Sax- ons, who began to settle the lands they had ravaged. In the course of all these conflicts, Roman culture and the Roman way of life dis- appeared from the British Isles.

Notable People

Antoninus Pius (86–161). Roman emperor, succeeded Hadrian. Ordered building of Antonine Wall between Forth and Clyde.

Boudicca, or Boadicea (died 62). Queen of the Iceni (East Anglian tribe), led revolt against Romans, sacked and destroyed Colchester, St Albans and London. Defeated, killed herself.

Gaius Julius Caesar (100–44 BC). Roman general and politician, conqueror of Gaul and eventual master of the Roman world. While in Gaul, made two expeditions to Britain.

Caractacus. Chieftain of Catuvellauni, led British resistance to Roman invasion of 43 AD. Captured in 50 AD and sent to Rome.

Cassivelaunus. British chieftain, main opponent of Julius Caesar's second expedition. Defeated, probably in a battle at Wheathampstead, near St Alban's.

Claudius (10 BC–AD 54). Roman emperor, decided on invasion of

England. Actual fighting conducted by his general, Aulus Plautius, but Claudius visited Britain to receive surrender.

Constantine the Great (died 337). Won control of Roman world after long series of wars. Made Christianity leading religion of empire. Founded Constantinople (now Istanbul, Turkey) as new capital.

Cunobelinus, or Cymbeline (died around AD 43). British chieftain, ally of Romans in period before invasion.

Hadrian (76–138). Roman emperor under whom empire reached its greatest extent. Great traveller.

Visited Britain in 122 and ordered building of 'Hadrian's Wall'.

Pelagius (died around 420). British monk, argued against doctrine of original sin, believing man could perfect himself. Church declared this a heresy. First British contribution to history of Christianity.

Life in Roman Britain

Population & settlement

The population of Roman Britain was perhaps half a million. For most of its history, Roman Britain ended at Hadrian's Wall, some miles south of the present English-Scottish border. But the Romans did venture further north, and in about AD 140 built an earthwork wall from the Forth to the Clyde (the Antonine Wall). It was finally abandoned towards the end of the second century.

Many peoples and races lived in Roman Britain. The army was drawn from all over the empire, from North Africa to Mesopotamia. Later, barbarian tribesmen were recruited in increasing numbers. Traders too seem to have come to settle in Britain from as far away as Syria.

Agriculture & food

The Roman occupation probably made little difference to most poor Britons, though they needed to grow enough to satisfy the Roman tax collector as well as their own needs. Corn-growing seems to have spread more widely, perhaps encouraged by opportunities to sell any surplus to the army. The growth of villas must have helped civilise the countryside. Large estates were owned directly by the emperor and worked by slaves; Their produce was mainly for export.

Meals followed Roman fashion. Guests lay down to eat, and drank wine with their food. However, a Celtic drink, beer, was also popular. The main meal, eaten late in the afternoon, consisted of hors d'oeuvres, one or more main courses and a sweet – very modern, in fact.

Towns, trade & industry

The first proper cities in Britain were built shortly after the Roman conquest. Cities were the basis of all Roman organisation, and they were planned with care. Sturdy walls protected them from attack. Streets were laid out on a sensible grid plan, criss-crossing at right-angles. A regular water supply was arranged, if necessary by building aqueducts. Drains and sewers were made, and rubbish was collected and buried. And at the heart of each city was the forum or city centre. This was a square surrounded by colonnaded (column-lined) buildings – the town hall, temples, baths, shops.

In the beginning, most British cities were closely connected with the army. Some were **coloniae** ('colonies'), which meant settlements of veterans who had served out their time. Others began with people who set themselves up outside garrison forts – wives and children, army suppliers, shopkeepers, entertainers. After the garrison left, the settlement carried on. London quickly became the chief British city, with York as the controlling centre in the north.

Multi-angular Roman tower at York

Chester and Caerleon were major garrison towns, and Carlisle, Wroxeter, Gloucester, Cirencester, Colchester, St Albans and Lincoln were all important centres.

Production and trade owed much to the army, which needed a constant supply of raw materials and goods, and could pay for them in cash. The coinage consisted of the brass sestercius, the silver denarius and the gold aureus, with values in the proportions 1:4:100. Later, after the economic crises of the third century, a new coin, the solidus, was introduced.

The chief industry was mining – of iron, lead, coal, tin, copper, and even gold, which was found in small quantities in Carmarthen.

Metals, corn and cloth were exported to other parts of the

Buildings

The Romans put up splendid public buildings in the cities of their empire. Roman town halls, temples, public baths and amphitheatres are still standing in a number of countries, but not, unfortunately, in Britain. There are many fragmentary remains, but nothing that gives an idea of the scope and solid grandeur of the Roman municipal style, with its many columns and round arches. From this point of view a good place to visit is probably the public baths at Bath.

The Romans were skilful engineers, practised in the use of stone,

Empire. Imports were mainly luxuries such as wine and 'Samian' pottery, though to Romanised Britons imported olive oil must have come to be a necessity of civilised life. Oil was used for massage after the baths, as well as in cooking.

15

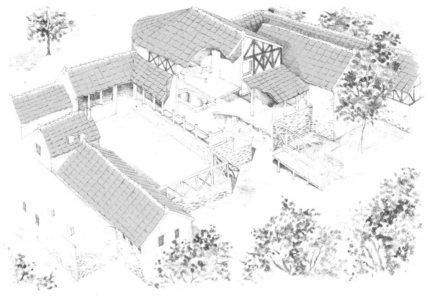

brick and concrete. In Britain they built aqueducts, forts, lighthouses and other structures, including Hadrian's Wall. Life in the country-side is known chiefly through the remains of villas, over 500 of which have been uncovered. These one-storey, stone-built farmsteads ranged from single buildings to luxurious complexes put up round an inner courtyard. Many villas were en-larged and improved over the cen-turies, which suggests that there must have been long periods of steadily increasing prosperity.

The finest villas, which had ex-pensive mosaic floors and private baths, may have been leisure homes rather than farms. A palatial ex-ample is the villa at Fishbourne, which was probably the combined home and political headquarters of Cogidubnus, the pro-Roman British king of the Regni.

But most villas were the centres of busy estates. The majority of those found so far are in southern and eastern England, where life was most secure. And in later centuries, many wealthy people left the towns and organised their estates so that they could be self-sufficient.

Interiors & furniture

Life in Roman Britain set new standards of comfort for the rich, and perhaps for a good many other people, at least in towns. Windows in villas had glass panes, keeping out draughts but letting in light. After the Romans left, there were no glass panes in Britain for a thousand years! Houses were centrally heated by means of pipes laid under the floors and leading from a furnace. Extra light was provided by candles or oil lamps made of pottery. Corridors gave greater privacy, making it possible to go from end to end of a house without passing through all the rooms. Furniture was upholstered and people slept on mattresses. Pottery, pewter and glass were widely used for eating and drinking. In towns people used public baths, which were a central part of the social life but in the countryside the wealthier villa-owners had baths installed. Some houses even had a form of flush lavatory. Decoration was provided by mosaics, hangings and wall paintings.

Clothing & appearance

The best-known Roman costume and one worn by both sexes, is the toga, a voluminous white woollen gown, wound round the whole body, with one end flung elegantly over the left shoulder. But the toga was not for everyday wear. It was the costume of the upper classes during important public and private ceremonies. For most of the time people wore one or more tunics or shifts and, then as now, cut and

materials depended on their ability to pay. Clips, bracelets, rings and other ornaments were worn by both sexes. Cloaks kept both men and women warm in winter, when they wore high boots rather than sandals.

Romans were clean-shaven up to the second century AD, after which beards became common. It is not likely that many women in

Roman dress consisted of a basic tunic covered by a toga for men or a stola for women

provincial Britain were fashionable enough to use make-up, but scent was known.

Social system

The most important differences were between Roman citizens, non-citizens who were free, and slaves. Citizenship was an honour, a privilege and an advantage. (In the New Testament, St Paul's Roman citizenship saves him from hasty trial and execution by his fellow Jews). Non-Roman soldiers who had served out their terms became citizens, and so did the king and chief men of British tribes who co-operated with the Romans. The other road to citizenship was to hold office as a magistrate.

After 214, when all free inhabitants of the empire were granted citizenship, wealth rather than class gave a man status and influence. Slaves were one form of wealth. A slave was property. He could be bought and sold, even if that meant separating him from his wife or children. There was a legal limit to the cruelty with which slaves could be treated, though it must have been hard to enforce. Most slaves must have been reasonably treated, if only to keep them working efficiently. Household slaves lived with the family that owned them, and were generally better-off than field-worker slaves. The slaves and convicts who worked in the imperial mines probably suffered most.

Government & justice

The governor of Britain was appointed directly by the Roman emperor, and answered only to him. But the important job of collecting taxes and paying the army was given to an independent official, the procurator.

In the third century, government was reorganised to cope with bar-barian attacks. Two governors were appointed, one to deal with civilian affairs and the other to supervise defence. Later, when the Saxon pirates had become the main threat, a new official called the Count of the Saxon Shore was appointed. He took charge of all the forts built along the east and south coasts, and of the soldiery there.

Within a few years of the Roman

A Roman-British kitchen in a big house, run by slaves. House slaves led quite a comfortable, privileged life by comparison with field slaves

conquest, only a few border areas were under direct military rule. In practice, the rest of Roman Britain was largely self-governing. The main divisions were the old tribal ones, but towns were the most vigorous centres. Each town was run by magistrates who presided in local courts, looked after public buildings and collected local taxes. The magistrates, who dealt with all minor crimes, were chosen by (and from) the town senate, a body elected from the wealthier inhabitants. Where the death penalty was involved, the governor, or a deputy, heard the case. The law was Roman law as it applied all over the empire, though Celtic custom may also have carried some weight.

War & defence

Britain was conquered by the famous Roman legions. These highly disciplined infantrymen were professional soldiers who enlisted for twenty-five years. Armed with a javelin (*pilum*) and a short stabbing sword (*gladius*), and massed behind a wall of big shields, they formed an almost irresistible military machine. By the time they came to Britain, the legionaries no longer came from Italy alone, but were drawn from all over the empire, from Spain to the Middle East.

Every legion was divided into ten cohorts, and every cohort into six centuries – bodies of a hundred men, each led by a centurion. Wherever the legionaries stopped, they built a camp or (for permanent garrisons) a fort. The engineering skills of the Roman army were often called upon in peacetime, when legionaries were employed to build many of the empire's great public works. And they also built great defensive structures such as Hadrian's Wall and the Antonine Wall.

By the third century, warfare had changed. Cavalry, once no more than an auxiliary, had become the dominant arm of the legions. Cavalry could move quickly from one place to another, defending the coasts threatened by Saxon pirates and relieving the forts that now dotted the 'Saxon Shore'.

throwing spear (pilum)

A Roman legionary

After the Roman armies left Britain, the Romanised Britons probably organised their own cavalry units. The Romans had often hired barbarians as cavalrymen, and the British followed their lead – at least if the story of Hengist and Horsa is true. They are said to have been Saxons hired by one of the British kings, Vortigern. He gave them lands on which to settle, but in time they turned on him and drove him from his kingdom. Possibly permanent settlement by the Saxons began in this way. Still, the British must have had their own units, for they resisted the Saxons long and bitterly.

Religion

The Romans were remarkably tolerant although they destroyed the druids of Britain, who practised

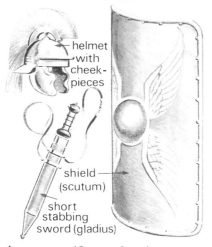

helmet with cheek-pieces

shield (scutum)

short stabbing sword (gladius)

human sacrifice, and at times persecuted Christians, who seemed dangerously pacifistic and refused to 'worship' the emperor. (A practice that showed loyalty to the emperor rather than a belief in his divinity.) On the whole, men might worship as they pleased. In Britain, the remains of altars and other evidence prove the presence of many religions. The old Celtic gods existed side by side with north- and east-European gods of barbarian auxiliary troops and with Jupiter and other Roman deities. Evidence of the Egyptian god Serapis has been found at York and the Persian god Mithras in London.

From 312, when Constantine gained control of the western empire, Christianity was favoured. By the fifth century it seems to have been widespread in Britain, surviving the departure of the Romans.

Right: Roman road over Wheeldale Moor, North Yorkshire. Diagram shows how the road was constructed

Communications

Communications improved tremendously in Roman Britain. Straight, wide roads linked the chief cities and garrisons. The best-known today are the Fosse Way (Lincoln - Leicester - Cirencester - Bath - Exeter) and Watling Street (Dover - Canterbury - London - Chester). Such roads were about five metres wide and were drained by a ditch on each side. They were made of layers of gravel, chalk and other materials – the result of careful surveying and long experience of military engineering.

Turf and Topsoil ▦ Gravel ▨ Flints ∞
Chalk rubble ▨ Chalk ⬚

A postal service carried official messages along them, if necessary as far as Rome itself. Many areas also had surprisingly large networks of minor roads.

Ports were developed and lighthouses made navigation safer. Dover lighthouse is particularly well preserved.

Education

Education must have been much the same in Britain as in other parts of the empire. The rich had private tutors for their children – often highly-educated household slaves. Other people (mostly those who were quite well off) paid to send their children to professional teachers. Both boys and girls might learn to read and to write, using a sheet of wax which could be smoothed down and used again and again. At about twelve years old, boys alone would go on to new studies, mainly literary and historical.

Art & ornament

At its best, Roman art was strikingly life-like, particularly in portrait sculpture and wall painting. But in Britain, the very edge of the Roman world, workmanship could be quite crude, especially on such objects as altars and tombstones.

Detail from mosaic floor at the villa-palace, Fishbourne, Sussex

The most interesting Roman-British survivals are floor mosaics – pictures made up of hundreds or thousands of small coloured stones.

The intricate Celtic style survived outside Roman Britain, and may not have been entirely forgotten inside the province. With the collapse of Roman rule, Celtic influences again became dominant.

A theatre in Roman Britain. Remains have been found in only a few towns; elsewhere people went to amphitheatres for cruder entertainments such as gladiatorial shows

Leisure

Many British pastimes began before the Romans arrived and continued for centuries after they left: hunting, dice, and cruel sports such as cock-fighting and bull- and bear-baiting.

The Romans introduced big public spectacles in the towns. They built theatres for plays and amphi-theatres for sports and fights. The theatre was in the open air, and consisted of a semi-circle of seats rising in tiers round a circular stage. Actors wore tragic or comic masks and specially built-up shoes to give them extra height. Many Roman plays are known, though none come from Britain.

Amphitheatres were also in the open, with tiers of seats stretching all round the arena. Both chariot racing and gladiatorial shows were popular everywhere in the empire. The gladiators were normally slaves; their career was gruesome and usually short-lived, but might also lead to fame and wealth. The standard contest was between the *mirmillo*, equipped with half-armour, sword and shield, and *retiarius*, with trident and net. But on great occasions whole armies of men and beasts, in varying combinations, were brought in to fight.

The public baths were among the most impressive buildings in Roman towns. They were not designed for swimming, but for thorough cleansing. With their steam rooms, cold plunges and masseurs, they were rather like modern Turkish baths. Most important of all, they were sports and social centres where people could lounge, gossip and play for hours. Even rich people did not bother with private baths in their town houses, preferring the sociability of the public rooms.

History on view

Small sections of Roman-British town walls can be seen in many places, including London. More impressive is the surviving stretch of wall and gate at **Colchester**.

Most of the more interesting Roman remains are in the south of England, where Roman-British life was most prosperous and secure. The **Fishbourne villa-palace**, for example, is near Chichester in Sussex.

Hadrian's Wall

Hadrians Wall

Detail from Great Dish found at Mildenhall

Roman baths, Bath

Mildenhall

Verulamium **Colchester**

LONDON □

Lullingstone

Bath

Dover

Fishbourne

A temple of Mithras was excavated in London in 1953. The find is preserved in the **Guildhall Museum**, London.

Pharos (lighthouse), Dover

Dover Lighthouse is a very exciting reminder of the far-flung imperial system of communications – though its rugged, dramatic look owes a lot to weathering!

Celtic shield of Roman period found at Battersea, London

The **British Museum** in London has a very large bronze head of Hadrian, rescued from the Thames. It evidently formed part of a colossal statue of the emperor. Nobody knows what became of the body. In the same museum, and also retrieved from the Thames, is a magnificent shield dating from the Roman period but as typically Celtic as Hadrian's head is typically Roman-realistic. The British Museum also holds the great silver treasure found at **Mildenhall**, Suffolk, in 1942.

Many mosaics are known, though all are more or less damaged. A well-known example is from **Lullingstone villa** in Kent.

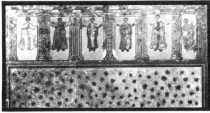

Wall-paintings from Lullingstone villa

There is a Roman theatre at **Verulamium**, outside modern St Albans. The leading resort in Roman Britain was **Aquae Sulis (Bath)** in Somerset, famous then and later for its hot springs, which were credited with health-giving powers. The city's Great Bath can still be visited.

Saxons, Scots and Vikings

Soon after the Romans left Britain, an age of great migrations and racial changes began. Angles, Saxons and Jutes from what are today North Germany and Denmark gradually conquered England (Angle-land), pushing back the British into the north and west.

At roughly the same time, another people, the Scots, were leaving their homes in Ireland and crossing over to the far north of Britain. As their territory spread, they absorbed the Picts, who disappeared completely in the ninth century.

Meanwhile, Christianity was carried by the western British into Ireland, and from Ireland into Scotland and northern England. The conversion of England was the joint work of this 'Celtic' church and missionaries sent by the pope in Rome. By the end of the seventh century the whole of the British Isles was Christian.

In the ninth century fierce Vikings from Denmark and Norway attacked and settled parts of England, Scotland and Ireland. But in time they were civilised, became Christians, and made their own special contribution to the history

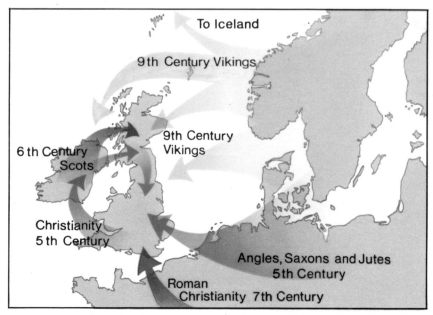

Map showing the movements of men and ideas in Anglo-Saxon times

A Celtic cross with distinctive wheel-shaped design at Earnley

Both Roman and Celtic churches took part in the conversion of the Anglo-Saxons to Christianity

of our islands.

England was divided into several kingdoms such as Mercia and Northumbria until the Viking invasions destroyed most of them. From one survivor, Wessex, grew a new and united English kingdom under Alfred the Great and his descendants. England became a stable, civilised land; even a period of Danish rule had little real effect on her. But the battle of Hastings in 1066, followed by the Norman Conquest, brought the Old English state to a sudden end.

Notable People

Alfred the Great (849–899). King of southern English state of Wessex, the only English state to survive Danish attack. The reconquest of England under Alfred's successors – Edward the Elder, Athelstan, Edgar – created a united monarchy.

St Augustine (died 604). Monk sent by Pope Gregory I to convert English. Baptised king of Kent. First archbishop of Canterbury.

St Bede, often called the Venerable Bede (673–735). English scholar who spent his life at Jarrow monastery. His *Ecclesiastical History* is a classic account of English church and people.

Brian Boru, or Boramha (926–1014). King of Ireland 1002–1014, ended Danish domination though killed at battle of Clontarf.

Canute, or Cnut (died 1035). Danish king of England 1016–1035, which he combined with Denmark and Norway in a short-lived 'northern empire'. Able and popular.

St Columba (521–597). Irish saint, chiefly responsible for conversion of Scotland.

St Dunstan (died 988). English monk, abbot of Glastonbury and later archbishop of Canterbury. Important leader of movement to reform and spread monasticism.

Edward the Confessor (died 1066). English king, founder of

Westminster Abbey. Devoted to religion, but a weak king.

Ethelred II (died 1016). English king remembered for efforts to buy off Norwegian and Danish attacks by paying 'Danegeld'.

Godwin (died 1053). Earl of Wessex and father-in-law of Edward the Confessor. Successfully opposed Edward when the king favoured Norman advisers. Most powerful man in kingdom. His son Harold was last Anglo-Saxon king of England, but was overthrown by William of Normandy in 1066.

St Patrick (died around 461). Of Roman-British family, converted much of Ireland to Christianity.

Life in Saxon Times

Population & settlement

Angles, Saxons and Jutes may have been separate peoples when they settled England, but they soon learned to think of themselves as a single people. The early differences are preserved in such names as East Anglia (land of the East Angles) and Sussex, Essex and Middlesex (lands of the South, East and Middle Saxons). We sometimes call these Germanic invaders 'English', sometimes 'Anglo-Saxons' and sometimes just 'Saxons'.

Historians are still arguing about how many Britons survived the Saxon invasions. What seems certain is that the survivors were lowly in status: 'Briton' was used by the English as a synonym for 'slave'. British language and culture disappeared in England without influencing the Anglo-Saxons, except in areas such as Cornwall and Cumbria which were conquered long after the rest. The Cornish language did not die out until the eighteenth century.

The pattern of Anglo-Saxon settlement was new. The British had farmed upland areas; the Anglo-Saxons settled in the valleys, doggedly breaking up the heavy soils. Over the centuries, slow but steady progress was also made in clearing the forests that covered England.

The Vikings (North or Norse men) were Scandinavians – mainly Danes and Norwegians. As a result of the ninth century invasions, eastern England and the Midlands were settled in great numbers by Danes. There were more Norwegians in Northumbria, and in the Western Isles of Scotland, which stayed under the control of the king of Norway. Both Danes and Norwegians settled on the east coast of Ireland, where there was the flourishing Norse kingdom of Dublin.

Agriculture & food

Over much of England agriculture was organised on the 'open field' system. The land of each village was divided into two, occasionally three, huge fields. Each year one of these was sown with spring and autumn crops while the other was left to lie fallow – that is, to recover from the sowings of the previous year. The fields were split up into many strips, each belonging to a particular family; one family might have several strips allocated to it, perhaps widely scattered.

Much of the work was organised as a communal effort, and even the teams of oxen were generally made up of animals belonging to several families. Village animals grazed on common wasteland and the peas-

Above: When Saxon invaders settled down, they began farming the English lowlands. They introduced the co-operative open-field system (inset) which in some places lasted into the eighteenth century

ants gathered fuel from the woods and made hay in the meadows. All the same, it was hard to provide enough food to keep animals alive during the winter, and many were killed and salted for later eating. But hunting and trapping must have supplied some fresh meat. The chief crops were cereals (wheat, oats, rye, barley), beans and peas. Ale was drunk.

Peasants in the south-west of England often owed services or rent to the local lord in return for their holdings. Their position worsened over the centuries, and many of them seem to have lost their freedom to move about or choose a new lord. In contrast, free peasants in the Viking areas managed to keep all their rights.

A good deal of English land was given over to cattle, pigs and sheep – wool was an important export – and in large areas of the less fertile Celtic territory, pasture was the rule.

Towns, trade & industry

The Roman towns of Britain fell into decay as Roman-British society declined. The Anglo-Saxons who succeeded them were a farming people and avoided towns. But local and national trade did gradually develop, and with it some towns. They also grew from the 'burghs', fortified places set up on King Alfred's orders as protection against the Danes. From this we get the word 'boroughs'.

In Scotland town life remained almost non-existent, and Ireland had no towns at all until the Vikings founded Dublin, Waterford and Limerick in the ninth century.

The most important industry in England was iron mining, the biggest centre being in the Forest of Dean. The iron trade flourished, for the metal was needed everywhere for ploughs and tools and also for weapons.

The Anglo-Saxons produced a fine coinage. The basic unit was the silver penny. There were 240 pennies to the pound, which remained the case until 1971!

Buildings

Most buildings of the time were made of wood. They have not survived, and little is known about them. In King Alfred's reign royal halls seem to have been made of stone and Anglo-Saxon monasteries and cathedrals were famous. But unfortunately only a few small churches, or rather parts of churches, have survived. These are notable for round arches and triangular windows and most of all for 'long and short work' – stones alternating between upright and horizontal.

The Church of St Lawrence, Bradford on Avon was built in the tenth century

Interiors & furniture

Very little is known. Accounts of

wealthy households mention rich hangings, bedding, tapestries, gold and silver goblets, cups, plates and bowls. Furniture must have been heavy and basic, for example massive long tables and benches, and chests that could double as seats, tables and bed-bases.

Clothing & appearance

Costume consisted basically of tunic and trousers for men. Women dressed in tunics and long skirts. Those who could afford it wore cloaks or mantles over this outfit. Materials included hides, wool and (for the rich) linen. Embroidery and jewelled brooches and clasps – not the cut of clothes – gave elegance. Men valued finely worked armour and weapons most of all.

Rough woollen clothes were worn by Saxon peasants

Social system

There were three classes in Anglo-Saxon England. The thanes were the wealthy, aristocratic class. The churls were free peasants who might be quite well off or could be very poor. Below the churls were slaves, who were property, with no rights at all.

Anglo-Saxon society kept many features of the warbands from which it had sprung. A chief who led in battle expected loyalty from his men, and was in turn expected to feast them and give them valuable gifts. This tradition was continued in the relations between lord and man when a settled society emerged. The lord gave his men land in return for service and loyalty, and his great hall remained a kind of social centre. He was responsible for his men in the eyes of the law and they were expected to support him in almost every situation.

The other important group to which men belonged was the kin – the family group. This included quite distant relatives and was also based on mutual support. In fact men pitied anyone who had no lord and no kin: he had no place in the world and no protection against attack or injustice.

Government & justice

Among the Celtic peoples, kings had little power in the face of tribal and

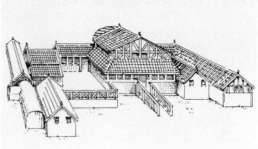

Above: Roman villas were skilfully built in stone but Saxon huts (left), built several hundreds of years later were primitive wood-built shelters

local loyalties. The situation was much the same in early Anglo-Saxon England. The country was divided into a number of kingdoms with only a nominal over-king or Bretwalda. But the Viking invasions destroyed the rivals of the kingdom of Wessex, which then expanded to become the kingdom of England.

Really important decisions were taken by the king and his council of chief men, the Witan. But most of the time the king ruled England like a great landlord, issuing orders and having accounts kept through his private household. King and household lived on the produce of royal estates. In addition there was royal income from 'farms' – a rent or tax on other estates, often paid in produce. And there was also a tax on every trading operation.

Taxes were collected by royal servants called ealdormen or, from Canute's time, earls. The ealdorman, usually a leading thane, controlled a county or town. We still use the word in the form 'alderman', and earls too are still with us. As well as collecting taxes, the ealdorman made sure that the peace was kept and that each area carried out its many duties.

As the powers of ealdorman expanded, lesser officers called reeves were appointed to administer taxes and run shires. The shire-reeve became 'sheriff', a title still used today.

In Anglo-Saxon England, direct government action was rare. Building forts and keeping bridges in repair, raising levies to fight and providing lodgings for the king's messengers – all such actions were the duty of local people, usually carried out in return for lands or privileges.

33

Vikings retreating behind a stockade. This was their standard tactic when they were hard-pressed on hostile ground

Much Anglo-Saxon law followed age-old custom, and men were often judged according to their reputations.

Punishments could be savage and hanging was known for very minor crimes. Many crimes or injuries were dealt with by fines. Injuries – even murder – could be atoned for by paying compensation, calculated on an elaborate fixed scale (*wergild*).

War & defence

There was no permanent Anglo-Saxon army. The king had a bodyguard known from King Canute's time as housecarls. But the defence of the country mainly rested with local levies – the *fyrd*, in which all free men were bound to serve.

Both Anglo-Saxons and Vikings retreated behind stockades when hard pressed. Alfred the Great created a whole system of *burghs* or forts which it was the duty of local people to keep in good repair.

The chief English weapons were spears and axes. Those who could afford them wore tunics of mail – sheets of small iron rings sewn on to fabric. Saxons fought on foot, but protected by a 'wall' of big shields they could ward off even the strongest attack. They lost the battle of Hastings only because they broke ranks and were run down by the Norman cavalry.

Religion

Ireland was converted to Christianity in the fifth century by St Patrick and other British missionaries.

Scotland became Christian in the sixth century, mainly through the leadership of an Irish monk, St Columba, who founded a monastery on the island of Iona.

England reverted to paganism as a result of the Anglo-Saxon conquest. The Christian British were pushed back into the far west and north; the invaders worshipped Woden and other Germanic gods. There is a huge, rather sinister hill figure on the Sussex Downs, the Long Man of Wilmington, which is probably meant to be Woden.

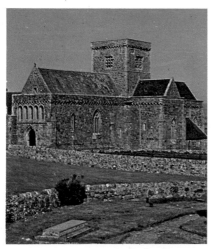

Monastery on the Scottish island of Iona, founded by St Columba in the sixth century

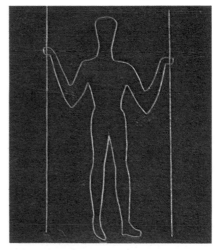

Long Man of Wilmington, Sussex. This design resembles those found on treasure from the Sutton Hoo

The re-conversion of England to Christianity was the work of missionaries from the Celtic and Roman churches. The two were not quite the same. The Celts, cut off from Europe, had developed different practices and a different form of organisation from the church led by the pope in Rome. For a time, it was not certain which church the Anglo-Saxons would join. The turning point was the Synod (church conference) of Whitby, at which the Northumbrian king decided in favour of Rome. Within fifty years the whole Celtic church itself had accepted Roman rule.

The seventh to eighth century was the great age of the Saxon church. Northern monasteries such as Lindisfarne and Jarrow became centres of piety and learning famous throughout Europe. Englishmen even became a force abroad, converting large areas of Germany to Christianity.

All this ended with the Viking invasions in the ninth century. The Vikings were pagans, and ruthlessly looted and destroyed religious houses. And though they agreed to be converted in 878 (after their defeat by Alfred the Great), other Northmen in Northumbria, Scotland and Ireland remained pagan until the tenth century.

This proved to be the last challenge to Christianity, and in the tenth and eleventh centuries the church flourished. Many churches were built by king or nobles, who kept the power of appointing the priest in charge (a practice that lasted into the twentieth century). Payments such as the tithe (tenth part of produce) became compulsory for everybody, and gave the church its income.

Communications

These were primitive in England and worse elsewhere. The Roman roads fell into disrepair as British society broke up, and at first they were little used by the Anglo-Saxons. The growth of towns and trade encouraged some repair of roads and bridges, which was a local duty. People travelled mainly on horseback. Any traveller who left the road was legally obliged to identify himself; if he failed to do so, the local inhabitants were entitled to assume he was up to no good and kill him on the spot. This kind of attitude towards strangers suggests that travel would not be undertaken lightly.

Education

Education was mainly run by and for the church, which needed priests and monks who could read and write Latin. Latin was the language of church services, and also the international language and the language of learning. The Anglo-Saxon church became known throughout Europe for its schools, its wealth of books and its fine scholars. The most famous religious centres were in the north – such places as York, Whitby, Wearmouth, Lindisfarne and Jarrow. But these suffered terribly from the Viking attacks, which began by destroying Lindisfarne in 793. Many precious books and other treasures were destroyed, and it was almost two centuries before Latin learning reached the same standard.

Meanwhile, English gained in importance. In the ninth century Alfred the Great made English a language of learning. He hoped that the whole Saxon upper class would eventually learn to read and write. A year-by-year record of events, the Anglo-Saxon Chronicle, began to be kept in the monasteries, and by the late tenth century many religious works were being written in English.

Art & ornament

Among the most mysterious of all remains are the Pictish symbol stones – boulders carved with symbols and lively figures of animals and men. Nobody knows what these stones were for, what the symbols meant, or even whether they are Christian or pagan. Later, many finely carved crosses were erected, especially in southern Scotland and northern England. The distinctively Celtic form was the wheel-headed cross.

Pictish symbol stones were carved with various symbols including animals, crescents, combs and mirrors. *Far left:* Stone from Broch of Birsay: *Left:* Stone from Fasterton of Roseisle, Morayshire (NATIONAL MUSEUM OF ANTIQUITIES OF SCOTLAND)

In Ireland, the monasteries of the Celtic church were famous centres of learning. They also excelled in one of the great European arts of the time: producing beautiful books. These 'illuminated manuscripts' are works of art, blending fine lettering with gold and brilliant colours, used in dense patterns. The *Book of Kells* is the best-known Irish example, but the Celtic style spread to Scotland and northern England, where the *Lindisfarne Gospels* were created.

Ornate purse-lid from Sutton Hoo treasure (BRITISH MUSEUM)

The Anglo-Saxons seem to have made magnificent embroideries, tapestries and metalwork for churches, palaces and weapons. Most of it has unfortunately been destroyed, but there is one great exception. At Sutton Hoo in Suffolk, archaeologists found a seventh century ship containing jewelled and enamelled dishes, weapons and other gear – probably buried as part of a king's funeral ceremonies. These early Saxon remains form the most splendid group of treasures ever found in the British Isles.

Left: The Sutton Hoo ship burial must have looked something like this. The treasure included silverware imported all the way from Byzantium (modern Greece and Turkey). There were also Merovingian (French) coins and ingots which helped to date the burial. *Below:* A detail from from the first leaf of the Book of Kells

Leisure

Hunting and hawking were traditional upper class pursuits, yielding fresh food as well as amusement. A good lord entertained his followers lavishly with food and drink in his hall. Inside and outside the hall, songs, poems, acrobatics and dice were popular pastimes. And the Anglo-Saxon poetic style, with its complicated kennings (name substitutes such as 'whale-road' for 'sea'), encouraged a great taste for riddles.

History on view

Frank's Casket, British Museum

Antiquities, Edinburgh. The *Book of Kells* is in **Trinity College Library,** Dublin. The *Lindisfarne Gospels* are in the **British Museum**, London, and so is the Sutton Hoo ship burial.

Lindisfarne Gospels, British Museum

The largest of Saxon remains is **Offa's Dyke**, which runs for about 190 kilometres between the Dee and the Severn. The dyke consists of a deep ditch and a high rampart. It would not keep out an invading army, but was probably intended to stop sporadic local fights and cattle raiding across a border – in this case the border between the Anglo-Saxon kingdom of Mercia and her Welsh neighbours. Offa was king of Mercia – and overlord of England – in the late eighth century. There are other substantial Saxon dykes in Cambridgeshire and Wiltshire.

One of the most impressive Saxon churches is **Brixworth**, near Northampton, which has a well-preserved tower and nave. There are other remains at nearby **Earls Barton**, at **Bradford-on-Avon** in Wiltshire, and at **Monkwearmouth** in Durham. The Saxon crypts at **Ripon** and **Hexham** are also well known.

Pictish symbol stones are best seen at the **National Museum of**

Crypt of Hexham Church

40

Edinburgh

Hexham
Monkwearmouth

Ripon

Dublin

OFFAS–DYKE

Brixworth
Earls Barton

LONDON

Bradford-on-Avon

Ripon Church, Yorkshire

The Normans fight their way up Senlac Hill at the Battle of Hastings. The Norman conquest changed the whole course of British history, strengthening the island's ties with Europe. *Inset:* Detail from the Bayeux tapestry, a copy of which can be seen at the Victoria and Albert Museum, London

Feudal Britain

In 1066 the Saxon army was defeated at Hastings by the troops of William, Duke of Normandy. The Saxon king, Harold, was killed in the fight. Duke William – 'William the Conqueror' – was crowned king of England, and his followers became the new ruling class.

Normandy is part of France. The new rulers, though descended from Vikings, were French in speech and outlook and at first were very much foreigners in England, holding down the Saxon majority. But over the following century the two peoples intermarried and gradually became one.

The Conquest brought really important changes – so much so that the period starting with 1066 is usually labelled 'the Middle Ages'. The Normans introduced a form of social organisation that was spreading over most of Europe. This was feudalism, with its division of society into nobles, knights and serfs.

Relations with Europe changed too. The long involvement with Scandinavia ended, to be replaced by close contact with western Europe. The English king was also duke of Normandy, and in the twelfth century added other parts of France to his possessions. There

were inevitable conflicts with the French kings, and a long series of Anglo-French wars began which went on for centuries. On the positive side, England became part of Europe and benefited from contact with new ideas and opportunities for trade.

For England, as for much of Europe, expansion was the keynote of the whole period. It was most marked in the twelfth century. Population increased, and vast areas of forest and marsh were cleared. Towns grew up and trade expanded. New and reformed monastic orders appeared, and learning flourished. In most areas of life there was greater comfort and refinement, at least for the better off.

The advances were greatest in the south and east of England. The north was much poorer, and suffered for generations from the 'harrying of the north' by William the Conqueror, carried out when he ruthlessly punished the 1069–70 Northern Rebellion. The rest of the British Isles was also poor and thinly populated, though in time it was also affected by the Conquest. Under Norman influence, Scotland adopted the feudal system in the eleventh to twelfth century. Wales was conquered and absorbed into the English state, and part of Ireland was seized. But the English effort to take over Scotland failed, and after the battle of Bannockburn, Scottish independence was assured.

Notable People

Roger Bacon (died 1294). English Franciscan friar, one of the earliest scientific experimenters in the modern spirit.

St Thomas à Becket (died 1170). English archbishop of Canterbury. Quarrelled with former friend Henry II over Church privileges; murdered by four of Henry's knights. Became saint; tomb in Canterbury Cathedral a popular object of pilgrimage.

Robert Bruce (1274–1329). King of Scotland 1306–29. Established independence against England.

Edward I (1239–1307). King of England 1272–1307. Great lawgiver. Conquered Wales. 'Hammer of Scots' – whom, however, he never quite succeeded in subduing.

Henry II (1133–89). King of England 1154–89. Also controlled much of France as duke of Normandy and Aquitaine. Strengthened legal system. First English king of Ireland.

John (died 1216). King of England 1199–1216. Lost Normandy; forced to sign Magna Carta.

Llewelyn the Great (died 1240). Prince of Wales, which he was fairly successful in uniting; maintained independence against English.

Llewelyn ab Gruffyd (died 1282). Prince of Wales, submitted to Edward I, rebelled, defeated, killed. Effective end of Welsh independence.

Simon de Montfort (died 1265). Norman-born English noble, led opposition to Henry III. Called historic parliament. Killed at battle of Evesham.

Richard I ('the Lion-Heart') (1157–99). King of England 1188–99, which he neglected for crusading exploits.

Sir William Wallace (died 1305). Scottish knight, led struggle for independence. Hunted down; hanged, drawn and quartered.

William the Conqueror (1027–87). King of England from 1066. Created strong monarchy. Ordered 'Domesday Book' survey of entire kingdom.

A later print of Henry II undergoing penance

Life in Feudal Britain

Population & settlement

In 1066 the English population was probably about 1,200,000, the Scots only 300,000, and the Welsh and Irish fewer still. By the end of the period the English population seems to have risen to well over 3,000,000.

The need for more food to feed the extra mouths encouraged a great movement of clearance and settlement in the twelfth to thirteenth century, though progress was delayed by the king's forest law. This prevented clearance of forest, or hunting in it, over large areas of the country – the object being to preserve game for the royal hunt and the royal table. As well as woodlands, marshes and fens were steadily pushed back in Somerset, Kent, Sussex and eastern England around the Wash.

Agriculture & food

The open field system carried on unchanged over much of England. But now most peasants were given a fixed status as villeins or serfs. This meant they were definitely no longer free – a situation foreshadowed in Anglo-Saxon times. They could not leave their land without their lord's permission, and in return for their holdings they had to work on the lord's land, usually for three days a week. The lord also received part of his serfs' produce, and they were burdened with various other payments and services. Use of the common continued, but if people obeyed the forest laws very many of them must have gone without fresh meat all winter. Poaching was probably widespread.

The typical settled area with open fields was called a manor. (Which is why the lord's house was the manor house – still quite a common placename.) The lord's private land was called his demesne. The so-called 'manorial system' covered much but by no means all of England, and outside England, societies remained generally poor and pastoral. In several parts of the country land was held separately and individually. And from the twelfth century, sheep farming became of great importance – not as a poor pastoral substitute for growing crops, but as a valued export supplying the textile industry of Flanders (roughly, modern Belgium).

There was little change in eating habits, except for the presence of one newcomer – the rabbit, brought into England from France during the twelfth century.

Towns, trade & industry

Medieval England was essentially a subsistence economy – in other words, one in which each settlement produced everything it needed to survive. Towns developed slowly as markets for surplus produce, as service-points for great castles and as centres of communication and administration. The great expansion of the twelfth century affected towns, which were often involved in a long struggle to win independence from a local lord; the town was most secure when a royal charter guaranteed its privileges. Chartered towns also began to appear in Scotland from the early twelfth century, at first populated by deliberately imported English merchants.

Inside towns, men of the same craft banded together in gilds. These were something like trade unions, but represented employers as well as workers: masters who ran their own workshops, the fully qualified

journeymen who worked for them and apprentices learning the job. With only limited work to be done, it was important for men in the same craft to stick together, stopping non-members (including 'foreign' craftsmen from other towns) from doing business in the town.

The main English export was wool. There was little industry apart from surface mining of coal and tin, but from the twelfth century windmills provided a new way of harnessing power. Later, water mills were adapted to fulling (beating and cleaning cloth), with very great economic effects in the following period.

The silver penny remained the basic unit of currency, but later in the period, the groat, worth fourpence, was introduced. Gold pennies were minted for a short time in the

Gild signs of medieval wool merchants

mid-thirteenth century but were
not a success.

Buildings

For their most imposing buildings,
the Normans used stone and concrete. This applied above all to
castles and cathedrals. Ordinary
parish churches were generally
made of wood until late in this
period.

Styles in church and cathedral
building changed with taste, and
with improvements in building
methods. The main styles were:
Norman (or Romanesque). Massively columned, with thick walls and
round arches and ceilings. Durham
Cathedral is a tremendously powerful and impressive example of the
style.
Early English. From the late twelfth
century. The first phase of a new
style, Gothic, the great style of the
European High Middle Ages. Pointed arches and ceilings, and tall,
narrow ('lancet') windows. Advances in building techniques made
it possible to raise ceilings and make
them span larger areas. This is
called vaulting. Lincoln and Salisbury Cathedrals are magnificent
examples of this style.
Decorated. From the late thirteenth
century. The second phase of
Gothic. A much more elaborate
style than Early English, with in-
tricately ribbed ceilings and big
windows, the top half filled with
exquisite, freely flowing tracery (a

Architectural changes illustrated by: Top,
Durham Cathedral (Norman); centre,
Salisbury Cathedral (Early English);
bottom, Ely Cathedral (Decorated)

patterned grid of iron, often holding stained glass). Exeter and Ely Cathedrals are of this period.

The houses of the wealthy and powerful developed first from castle design. As life grew more secure, heavy fortification began to seem unnecessary, though many large houses kept a rather castle-like appearance for centuries. Stokesay Castle is a fine surviving example.

Ordinary people's houses ranged from miserable shacks to substantial stone town houses; one of these still standing is the impressively sturdy 'Aaron's House' in Lincoln.

Interiors & furniture

At the time of the Conquest even a baron's house was basically a single room – the old Great Hall, covered in rushes, where masters and servants ate and slept together. The Norman Great Hall at least had alcoves set aside for the master and his family, and these developed into separate sleeping quarters. In the castle, the Great Hall was on the first floor (for additional security), and this layout was followed in early manor houses. Outside stairs – which could be blocked or destroyed in an emergency – led directly to the hall. The ground floor was used for stores, and perhaps for kitchens.

Windows let in light, but also draughts and rain. Glass was not used, and though wooden shutters kept out the worst weather, they made interiors dim and stuffy.

Towards the end of this period, flues and chimneys began to replace the simple hole in the roof as a way of getting rid of smoke.

Clothing & appearance

With draughty houses and inefficient heating, it is not surprising that medieval clothing was generally long, thick, multi-layered and often fur-lined. In fact most forms of costume, for both men and women, can be summarised as tunics (cotes) worn under larger tunics (surcotes or tabards; kirtles for women). These might be covered by a cloak, or by the even more voluminous pelisse. Long stockings or bandage-like leggings were worn with heel-less leather or wool shoes. Peasants wore shorter tunics for work, and clogs as overshoes when working in muddy conditions.

The Normans wore their hair very short, often shaving their heads at the back. Later, hair was worn curled just below the ears, with a fringe at the front. The hood (capuchon) covered both head and shoulders very efficiently. When not being used it formed a triangle on the wearer's back. Women usually wore a veil or mantle that fell to their shoulders, hiding their hair. Later this became the smaller wimple, a piece of linen wound round the head under a cap or other headdress. (Wimples are still worn by some orders of nuns.)

Social system

Feudalism was a system in which a man held land in return for service – which might mean fighting, praying or working on the land. In theory the king owned the whole country, but he distributed most of the land among his barons. Each baron accepted the king as his lord and accepted certain obligations – in particular, to provide so many knights to serve the king in wars, processions, and at court, for specified periods each year.

Barons who held their lands directly from the king were called tenants-in-chief. They in turn gave land to tenants who became their vassals: they took the baron as their lord and agreed to serve or provide knights for the royal or baronial courts. The knights themselves would be given land in return for service.

The care taken to ensure an adequate supply of knights emphasises their decisive role in warfare. But in the long run the system proved rather clumsy; sometimes knights who had served the agreed time went home in the middle of a campaign. So money payments (scutage) gradually replaced service; in effect, lords and knights tended to become country gentlemen, paying rents to the king, who could use this income to hire professional soldiers.

The feudal system can be seen as a kind of pyramid, with the king at the apex and the peasants at the base, providing the food supply. Many peasants were serfs, halfway between outright slaves and free men. On the other hand, slavery itself soon died out. For slaves, becoming villeins was an improvement in status and rights.

The church too was an important part of the feudal system. Bishops and abbots were often great land-owners, owing and extracting service like other magnates. And all peasants were obliged to pay a tithe – a tenth part of produce – to the church for its upkeep.

Feudalism in Scotland dates from the reign of David I (1124-53), who imitated English practice to the extent of importing his own Norman followers.

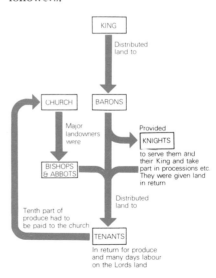

Diagram to show how the feudal system worked

Government & justice

The king ruled England as a great landlord might administer his private estate. He travelled round the country living off his demesne and hunting in the forests. His day-to-day 'government' was carried on by members of his household, which only gradually became a proper civil service based at Westminster.

Important decisions were taken by the king with the advice or consent of his Great Council, the *Curia Regis*. His most trusted servants and the great men of his realm attended. Later, the Great Council was more often called a parliament. During the troubled reign of Henry III (1216-72), Simon de Montfort decided to call a parliament and tried to get extra support for his policies by summoning representatives from the well-off but non-aristocratic classes. Two knights came from each county, and two burgesses from each city or borough. From these – 'the commons' – eventually developed the House of Commons which is the heart of the British parliamentary system.

Magna Carta was also a landmark. It was primarily a technical document, defining feudal rights, but it did guarantee certain freedoms. And above all it confirmed that English kings could not be despots, but were bound by English law and custom.

However, it was finally the great nobles who carried most weight in the land, and the personal relations between them and the king determined how successfully the country was governed. Thanks to William the Conqueror, the English monarchy was relatively strong – certainly stronger than the Scottish, let alone the Irish and Welsh, which were no more than vague overlordships. But the personality of the king was a decisive factor: a weak or unpopular king would fail to control the baronage and almost certainly find himself faced with rebellion or civil war.

Local government was dominated by the sheriff who controlled the courts of his shire, ran the royal demesne and headed the local militia (*fyrd*).

The complicated network of feudal obligations made for frequent litigation (going to law) over many questions. Lawyers developed into a single profession, and towards the end of the period the famous Inns of Court were established in London as lodgings and study centres.

King John was forced to accept the terms of the Magna Carta which he signed at Runnymede in 1215.

A copy of the charter can be seen in the British Museum

Feudal England had many courts: royal and baronial courts, church courts, and local shire and hundred courts continued from Anglo-Saxon times. But the great feature of the age was the expansion of royal justice under Henry I and Henry II, The Common Law, based on experience of past cases (precedent), emerged as the main English system. It was administered by travelling justices and great courts such as King's Bench. However, the church remained outside royal control.

Punishments remained simple and severe. The pillory and the stocks were used for minor offences, and trial by ordeal, and hanging, drawing and quartering were introduced.

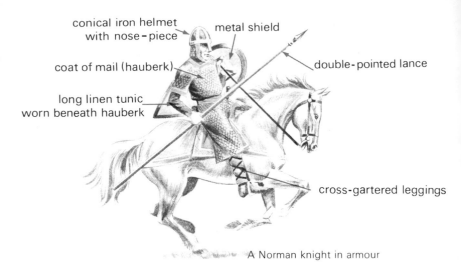

conical iron helmet with nose-piece

metal shield

coat of mail (hauberk)

double-pointed lance

long linen tunic worn beneath hauberk

cross-gartered leggings

A Norman knight in armour

War & defence

This was an age of heavyweights. The chief means of defence was the castle, which grew more massive with each century. The main mobile unit was the knight, whose weapons, armour and powerful horse gave his attack a smashing, nearly irresistible impact. Armoured man and horse made up the supreme fighting machine of the age – a sort of medieval tank. This comparison also gives a fair idea of the great expense involved in getting and maintaining man, horse and equipment. That, of course, is why knight service was so important in feudal arrangements.

Poorer countries could not afford knights. Scotland relied mainly on spearmen, arrayed in semi-circular formation (the *schiltron*). The Irish followed the Norse tradition of fighting with the axe; axemen from the Western Isles called 'gallowglasses' were imported as mercenaries for centuries and many of them settled in colonies in the north.

Religion

Conflicts flared up between king and church from time to time. One issue was the independence of church courts; another was the power of appointment to positions in the church, which was eventually settled by a compromise between king and pope. The issue was an important one for the king: appointing his own men to clerical office was a good way of controlling the church – and also an economical way of paying state servants.

The greatest religious movement

of the age was monastic. Hundreds of houses were founded in the twelfth century, almost all from new, strict orders, among them Cluniacs, Cistercians and Carthusians. All three came from the Continent, but the most important, the Cistercians, was co-founded by an Englishman, Stephen Harding. The Cistercians embodied the urge to retreat from the world, building their abbeys in wild, faraway places. In the thirteenth century the Friars arrived, motivated by the opposite ideal – to live a life of poverty and spirituality in the heart of the world.

Communications

There was plenty of travelling in the early Middle Ages. Kings and nobles moved from estate to estate, justices went 'on circuit' and pilgrims and traders made long journeys. But conditions remained primitive, even at their best in southern England. Roads and bridges were still a local responsibility. Travel was on foot or on horseback; ladies might be carried in litters, and carts were used for carrying heavy goods, but roads were usually too muddy, rutted and bumpy for carriages. There were few inns, and one of the important functions of monasteries was to provide security and hospitality. Still, people preferred to travel by water if they could.

Early print of carriage used during the reign of King John

Education

The Conquest made French the language of the court, the aristocracy and literature until the thirteenth century when gradually a new English emerged, blending French and Old English and spoken by the whole people.

Latin remained the international language and the language of learning. There were still few people outside the church who could read or write, including the nobility. But there was some spread of literacy through schools, which were set up under licence from a bishop.

During the twelfth century groups of scholars settled in Oxford to study. In 1264 Walter de Merton founded a hall where they could live and work together, and this became the first college of Oxford University. Cambridge University was founded soon afterwards.

Art & ornament

A great deal of early medieval art was carried out for the church: illuminated manuscripts, wall paintings (very few have survived), stained glass, ornamental carvings and sculptures in wood and stone. These were not separate arts in the modern sense, but were closely connected with the dominant building styles.

All art forms reached a peak of dazzling ingenuity in the early fourteenth century. Many ornamental details of the great cathedrals are superb miniature works of art, for example, capitals (heads of columns) and misericords (grotesques carved on the undersides of tip-up seats).

Very little secular (non-religious) work survives; most gold and silver work, for example, has been melted down at some time.

Leisure

The pastimes of the poor were

Left: Boar-hunt in the Middle Ages. Hunting was not just a sport but an important source of food, and for this reason the upper classes tried to monopolize it for their own benefit

Above: 'The Lady of Shalott' by John William Waterhouse, illustrated a famous poem based on a tale from the Arthurian legend (TATE GALLERY)

cheap and simple, such as athletics and wrestling. Gambling with dice was enjoyed by all classes, so were chess and draughts. Brutal sports such as bull- and bear-baiting and cock-fighting remained popular for several centuries after this period.

Hunting was the sport of the rich. The king hunted in his forests and the nobles in their deer-parks. In this way they kept themselves in training for war and provided a supply of fresh meat.

Tournaments too were really re-hearsals for warfare. In fact they were miniature battles between 'armies' of knights – dangerous affairs and likely to start feuds. In the thirteenth century they began to be replaced by the more civilised Round Table. This is what most people now think of when they talk about tournaments – a series of jousts between individuals using blunted weapons. They were part of a growing cult of chivalry which found its most romantic expression in the legend of King Arthur.

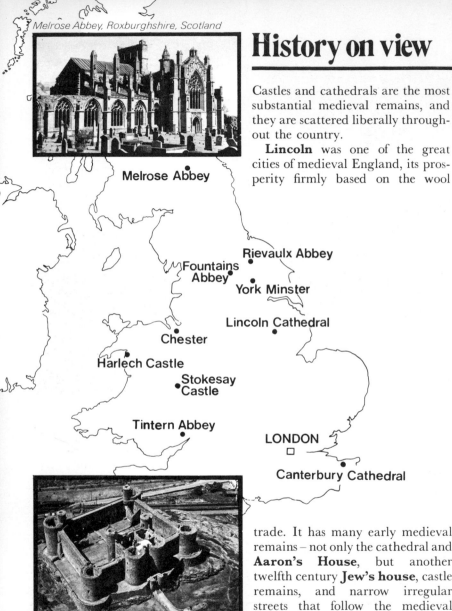

Melrose Abbey, Roxburghshire, Scotland

History on view

Castles and cathedrals are the most substantial medieval remains, and they are scattered liberally throughout the country.

Lincoln was one of the great cities of medieval England, its prosperity firmly based on the wool

Melrose Abbey

Rievaulx Abbey

Fountains Abbey

York Minster

Lincoln Cathedral

Chester

Harlech Castle

Stokesay Castle

Tintern Abbey

LONDON

Canterbury Cathedral

trade. It has many early medieval remains – not only the cathedral and **Aaron's House**, but another twelfth century **Jew's house**, castle remains, and narrow irregular streets that follow the medieval layout.

At **Chester**, medieval walls are

Harlech Castle, Wales

Lincoln Cathedral

Cistercian abbeys were built all over the British Isles, but because they were sited in remote places, they fell into ruins after the dissolution of the monasteries. Even as ruins they are worth visiting. Famous examples are **Fountains Abbey** and **Rievaulx** in Yorkshire, **Tintern Abbey** in Gwent, and **Melrose** in Scotland.

to be seen, as well as the famous 'rows', first-floor walks and shops. The remains of walls at **York** are particularly fine.

Stokesay Castle is in Shropshire.

Stokesay Castle, Shropshire

Fountains Abbey, Yorkshire

Most stained glass from this period has been destroyed, but there are some fine examples in Canterbury Cathedral, and some of the glass at York Minster dates from the twelfth century.

York Minster and City Wall

The Later Middle Ages

The feudal age had been one of rapid advance on all fronts. But in the later Middle Ages things were less clear. The boom in agriculture started to taper off – and was then utterly destroyed by the Black Death, a terrible plague that ravaged Europe.

This disaster did give rise to improvements in the peasants' lot. It hurried on the end of feudalism, giving the peasants much more freedom. Attempts were made to stop this happening, and the Peasants' Revolt of 1381 was brutally put down. But in spite of this setback, working conditions generally improved. Wages rose, and in the countryside a great new cloth industry grew up.

The middle classes also became more prosperous and important. But leadership remained with the great lords in both politics and war. The Hundred Years War with France (actually 1338–1453) witnessed brilliant English victories (at Crécy, Poitiers and Agincourt) and a new sense of English unity and national pride. All the same, the final result of the wars was the loss of all English territories in France except Calais.

The end of this old involvement may have been a good thing, but defeat weakened the prestige of the crown at a difficult moment. With the feeble king Henry VI on the throne, the nobility formed themselves into rival parties – at first for control of the crown, and later to fight over who should actually wear it. The Wars of the Roses, though interrupted by quite long periods of stable government, made late fifteenth century life seem very insecure. Few people can have guessed, when Henry VII won the throne in 1485, that a new age had begun.

The Black Death, or bubonic plague, swept through Europe. Although people believed the infection could be breathed in, it was in fact carried by the fleas of the black rat; bad hygiene, especially in the crowded little towns, helped the plague spread

Border warfare between the English and the Scots carried on – officially and unofficially – throughout the whole period. English rule in Ireland weakened, and by the fifteenth century only Dublin and the surrounding 'Pale' remained.

Notable People

William Caxton (died 1491). English merchant who learned the art of printing in Germany and set up the first English press at Westminster in 1476.

Geoffrey Chaucer (died 1400). First great modern English poet; wrote *The Canterbury Tales*.

Edward III (1312–77). King of England 1327–77, claimed French crown and began Hundred Years' War against France. Despite brilliant victories, reign ended in disappointment.

Edward, the Black Prince (1330–76). Eldest son of Edward III, won famous victories at Poitiers and in Spain. Died before his father. The Black Prince's son became king as Richard II.

Edward IV (1442–83). King of England 1461–69 and 1471–83, first of Yorkist line. Did much to strengthen monarchy but left only a child (Edward V) as heir.

Henry IV (1367–1413). King of England 1399–1413 following rebellion against Richard II (deposed). First Lancastrian king.

Henry V (1387–1422). King of England 1413–22. Defeated French at Agincourt, conquered large territories; recognised as heir to French throne but died young.

Henry VI (1421–71). King of England 1422–61; 1470–71. Pious, but weak and not always sane. Reign troubled by loss of France and civil war (Wars of the Roses).

Richard III (1452–85). King of England 1483–85, brother of Edward IV. Usurped throne from boy Edward V and is reputed to

have ordered murder of Edward and his brother. Defeated by Henry Tudor and killed at Bosworth.

Wat Tyler (died 1381). Leader of the Peasants' Revolt with the priest John Ball. Stabbed to death during conference with Richard II.

The Earl of Warwick, 'the Kingmaker' (1428–71). Most powerful of all fifteenth century magnates. Played great part in making Yorkist (Edward IV) king, and then in bringing him down; defeated and killed on Edward's return to power.

John Wycliff (died 1384). English scholar at Oxford, wrote in favour of religious reforms and started translation of the Bible into English.

Medieval Life

Population & settlement

In England, the Black Death killed about a third of the population. The plague returned again and again for centuries and population recovery seems to have begun only at the end of the period.

A fall in population meant a fall in the number of workers and also in demand for food. Less productive land tended to go out of cultivation, or else to be turned over to sheep farming. The great prosperity and rising population of the thirteenth century had encouraged new settlements on lands that only just paid their way. As a result of the Black Death more than a thousand villages in England alone were abandoned and vanished. Most of them have been identified by historians only in the last few years.

The plague struck hardest in towns, where large numbers of people were crowded together. For this reason its effects were probably less serious in Scotland and the rest of the 'Celtic fringe'.

Agriculture & food

Farming methods changed little, but the social system in the countryside was revolutionised, mainly by the Black Death.

Serfdom ended. With a smaller population, labour was scarce and wages therefore rose, while food prices remained static or even fell. More land given over to sheep-farming may also have meant a higher-protein diet for the workers. In general, wage-labourers were better-off than in the period before or the period after this one.

Towns, trade & industry

As the Black Death hit hardest in the towns, some medieval centres, such as Lincoln, began to decline, but many towns recovered surprisingly quickly. By the fifteenth century, London was already far and away the largest and busiest place in Britain. Bristol also grew rapidly with new opportunities for trade outside Europe. Other towns, such as Coventry, Leeds and Halifax, benefited from the great new cloth industry.

In the early fourteenth century, wool was still the main English export. But the introduction of the fulling mill completely changed the situation. Englishmen became weavers and sold the finished cloth instead of the raw wool abroad. Weaving was a country industry, done wherever sheep and streams were found together. It brought new prosperity to the West Riding of Yorkshire, the West Country, Suffolk and the area around Coventry.

Fifteenth century manuscript showing early spinning and weaving techniques

In general, European trade became less important, but local trade thrived. The gilds, formed in feudal times, reached the peak of their power and influence. A small-scale shipping trade flourished all down the coast between Newcastle and London, helped by the coal mined in the Tyne area and brought south by sea. Coal was not yet used in the home, but was valued for craft and industrial use.

Buildings

The most magnificent buildings were still those erected by the church. From the mid-fourteenth century the dominant style was Perpendicular. This was the third and final stage of Gothic, and was a purely English development. In other countries Gothic became more and more elaborate, but Perpendicular gave up free-flowing tracery for emphatic straight lines, both vertical and horizontal. The age of cathedral-building was over, but the new style was used for rebuilding, and for building hundreds of new churches. In some of the more ambitious Perpendicular buildings, for example King's Chapel, Cambridge, the walls are nearly all windows of stained glass, with just a stone grid holding the windows together. The other great feature of Perpendicular was fan vaulting – beautiful patterns of radiating ribs covering the ceiling. By the late fifteenth century these had developed into stone pendants which seem about to drip from the vault, as in Henry VII's Chapel, Westminster.

Castles were still built in England, and the growing number of country houses often had military features, but this was mainly for show. From the fourteenth century bricks were increasingly used for such houses. Near the Scottish border, however, and in Scotland and Ireland, life was less secure and building reflected this. A characteristic form of defence was the round tower – basically a cheap ' version of the castle, like an unprotected keep.

English and Scottish examples are called peel (or pele) towers.

Interiors & furniture

Life was probably more comfortable for all classes in England. Great lords maintained enough men to make the hall still the centre of the house or castle. But other wealthy and well-born people tended to have smaller halls and more private rooms. Glass, chimneys and carpets were still the possessions of a small minority. Some furniture was finely carved, and in noble households the sideboard became an important item for displaying plate.

Clothing & appearance

In the later Middle Ages, fashion in the modern sense began. Clothing for the upper classes was skilfully

The Chapel of King's College, Cambridge

tailored, often in order to show off certain features. Tunics, for example, were made short, tight and shaped, displaying the waist, while ladies' gowns might be low-cut, or slashed at the sides. Colours became

Clothing for the rich became tailored, and bright coloured, fine cloths such as velvets and brocades became popular. The poor (lower picture) also became better dressed, their woollen garments were dyed in attractive colours

brighter and materials more varied – linen, muslin, brocades, velvets, gold and silver tissue, furs.

Styles changed rapidly and became ever more fanciful, involving pleating, padding and stiffening. Men wore great puff sleeves, and women gowns that trailed along the floor. Long, voluminous clothes, often fur-lined, provided a common-sense note – and the necessary warmth. Shoes became longer and more pointed – so much so that some men's shoes had to be tied to the knees of their stockings. Hats were often beautiful, but impossibly tall and elaborate.

Curiously enough, the men who dressed so extravagantly wore their hair in the most basic of styles – the pudding basin, thick on top but shaved right round the head in a line above the ears.

The dress of people below the ruling class seems to have improved too. Previously peasants had worn 'hodden grey' (undyed, very coarse woollen cloth) because they had no choice. When they grew more prosperous, they bought better and brighter clothes. Parliament tried to stop this happening by passing laws which laid down what the various classes might wear but they couldn't be put into practice. The idea that a peasant might be mistaken for a gentleman was horrifying – to everyone but a peasant. Possibly the extravagant and impractical upper-class fashions were designed to discourage imitators!

Social system

Feudalism linked service with land-holding, but in the later Middle Ages money became the most important means of payment, both for service and as rent. The great lords kept their leadership in war and society, but they now led their troops in return for pay, and in turn paid their followers and recruits.

As landowners the nobles found it profitable to lease their lands – again in return for money rents. In this way the great estates were broken up among farmers of middling wealth. The middle classes seem to have flourished in this period, and on the land three types emerged: the gentry, the yeomen and the husbandmen.

These 'titles' were very loosely used, but their meaning was roughly as follows:

The gentry employed other people to do the manual work on their lands, had some education and displayed a coat of arms.

Yeomen farmed at least enough land to keep themselves and their families in solid comfort. They might be employers, but might also work side by side with their labourers. Some yeomen were richer than some gentlemen, but were less socially ambitious.

The husbandmen had land to farm, but not necessarily enough to support them without doing some work for other people.

Below these were villagers who worked their strips in the open fields; cottagers with little more than a garden plot, and a growing mass of day labourers who worked for pay.

After the Black Death labour was scarce, and serfs were gradually able to refuse the old feudal services and become free peasants, renting their lands and/or working for pay.

Government & justice

Central government was still limited in scope, but the administration became settled and separate from king and court – became, in other words, a civil service.

But the king's personal qualities were still decisive. A king's effectiveness depended on the co-operation of the magnates. A popular king – especially a warrior king like Edward III   could get away with a good deal. An unpopular or weak one might be deposed and murdered, like Edward II, Richard II and Henry VI. In the later Middle Ages the magnates tended to control the king's council, which gave them more power than in the feudal period. On the other hand, effective royal control of the church established, partly thanks to the scandal of the Great Schism. While rival popes quarrelled, English kings chose bishops and other churchmen.

Parliament developed something like its modern structure, with the lords and the 'commons' – knights and burgesses – sitting separately. Acts of 'the king in parliament' had a certain solemn force, as representing the whole property-owning community. However, in the fifteenth century Parliament was generally controlled by one or other faction of great lords, who used it for their own ends.

The limits on all late medieval authority are shown by the failure of laws that large numbers of people did not want to obey: such as the laws to fix wages and to lay down what people should wear.

In local government, the sheriff became less important. The justice of the peace (JP), normally a member of the local gentry, was given a very wide range of powers, acting as unpaid police chief, judge and economic overseer, fixing prices and validating weights and measures. For much of the period, however, JPs were followers of the magnates who dominated most localities, and manorial courts still played a part in the legal system.

The law became an ideal profession for the younger son of good family who would not inherit his father's estate.

War & defence

Although most holders of knights' fees had become peaceful country gentlemen, military tradition was still strong among the nobility. But now, instead of giving feudal service, nobles worked on contract for pay; and they in turn paid those they recruited. However, in emergencies the local levies were called out more and more often.

One reason for this was that the armoured and mounted man no longer decided the outcome of wars. At Crécy and other battles, archers – peasants armed with longbows – carried the day. The longbow, sometimes nearly two metres in length, could be fired with great rapidity (unlike the professional soldier's crossbow). A company of archers could rain arrows on the enemy without stopping – killing many and demoralising the rest.

As a result, military tactics changed. Knights now often fought on

66

The Battle of Crécy was a crushing defeat for France. New weapons such as the longbow, and later gunpowder, were to end the long supremacy of the knight in armour. *Below:* This fifteenth century complete armour, in the Wallace Collection, London, weighed just under 100 lbs

foot, grouped as a defensive mass and flanked by archers. Equipment improved: chain mail was replaced by plate armour, so skilfully jointed that the wearer could move about with some ease.

But in the long run it was gunpowder which transformed the face of war. Though used from the fourteenth century, early guns were not very effective. Cannons were very expensive to make, and there were so few that they were given names, like the famous Mons Meg in Edinburgh. But by the late fifteenth century, artillery could batter down castle walls, making obsolete the great defensive works of the Middle Ages.

Religion

There were striking changes in Christian practice and belief. Much greater devotion was shown to the Virgin Mary and the saints, in the hope that they would take the sinner's part in Heaven. For much the same reason, people who could afford it paid for chantries – chapels where priests said prayers for the souls of dead relatives and friends. And poorer people often bought indulgences – certificates that were believed to shorten the time a man must spend in purgatory, where sinners suffered and were purified before being allowed into heaven.

It was not a great age for the church itself. There was generally less zeal than in earlier times, and no new orders were founded. Various abuses existed; priests often held several benefices, and many bishops never visited their sees.

Most people did no more than grumble about this sort of thing. But some developed quite revolutionary ideas, and were branded as heretics by the church. One was the Oxford scholar Wyclif, whose example encouraged the Lollard movement. The Lollards challenged

A later print of Henry V attacking a Lollard meeting

the authority of the church by claiming that each man – not the church – was the best judge of scripture and his own actions. Their following was particularly strong among middle and lower-middle class people in the towns, until many were burnt at the stake in the reign of Henry V. Lollards survived here and there, but were forced into secrecy.

Communications

Travel seems to have become more frequent, and there were more inns at which travellers could pay to stay the night. Other conditions changed little.

Education

English now became the language of the whole people, although scholars continued to use Latin.

There were great advances in education. The nobility and many of the gentry sent their children to schools; the first of the great to read and write. In the towns, gilds were active in founding schools; The first of the great grammar schools were founded – Winchester in 1382, Eton in 1440. The earliest English family letters date from the fifteenth century, and about a third of the population may have been literate. Progress was slower in Scotland, but the first university, St Andrew's was founded in 1410.

Eton College – one of the first public schools

The introduction of printing promised even greater advances. Until the fifteenth century the way to increase copies of a book was to have it written out again and again. So much labour made a book a luxury object – and, indeed, illuminated manuscripts were often works of great beauty. Printing multiplied copies quickly and efficiently. It heralded a world in which knowledge and ideas would be available to all who could read.

Art & ornament

Secular art became more important in this period. Illuminated manuscripts, for example, were not just made for the church; nobility and gentry liked lavish books of hours (books of prayers for set times of the day) in particular. The *Luttrell Psalter* is by no means the best religious illuminated manuscript,

Detail from the Syon Cope, a beautiful example of medieval embroidery
(VICTORIA AND ALBERT MUSEUM, LONDON)

but it is remarkable for its scenes of everyday life. In general, artists combined realism with charm, especially in recording animals and birds.

In the fourteenth century English embroidery became famous throughout Europe as *Opus Anglicanum*, delicate but opulent in the use of gold, silver and coloured thread. Carvings in alabaster were also exported. The material is very hard, and lent itself to the kind of realistic detail that the age admired. Tombs and tomb effigies could be splendid, though many were mediocre – mass-produced to a pattern in (mainly) London workshops.

One of the supreme achievements must have been in stained glass design, carried out in a far greater range of colours than before. Unfortunately most windows of the time have been destroyed, but there is magnificent stained glass at York Minster.

Leisure

There was little change. Under Edward III, the tournament became more spectacular, stricter in its rules and therefore rather less dangerous. The cult of chivalry reached its height. Ironically, this happened when the feudal system and the absolute supremacy of the knight were disappearing.

Plays or shows probably existed in some form before this period, but the first lengthy, recorded examples were now produced. Most gilds put on their own 'miracle' or 'mystery' (craft or occupation) plays, usually based on Bible stories. The fifteenth century 'morality play' had a new emphasis, dealing with everyday life, though with religious emphasis and abstract characters such as Pride, Knowledge and Greed.

The longbow proved such a deadly war weapon that archery was made compulsory by law. The rough, early forms of football and golf, on the other hand, were forbidden by royal proclamation in both Scotland and England – evidently without much effect. The chief new pastime was playing cards, which appeared in England in the mid-fifteenth century. (The 'court cards' still show fifteenth century dress.)

Miracle and morality plays were performed on makeshift stages in churches, market places and inn yards. There was nothing solemn about these performances, in which there was plenty of dialect and earthy humour

History on view

Westminster Abbey, London

Perpendicular churches are so common that most people live near one or more. In **Westminster Abbey** it is interesting to compare Henry VII's Chapel with the east end and nave, which are in the Early English style. There are a number of well-

Peel Tower, Narrow Water Castle, County Down

preserved peel towers, especially in Northumberland and Down, Northern Ireland. **John Knox's house** in Edinburgh dates from the fifteenth century.

There are splendid examples of late medieval armour on show in the **Wallace Collection**, London. **Mons Meg** stands on the battlements of Edinburgh Castle.

The Luttrell Psalter is in the **British Museum**, London. **The Syon Cope**, a superb piece of **Opus**

Luttrell Psalter, British Museum

Anglicanum, is in the **Victoria and Albert Museum**, London. An alabaster effigy of Edward II is the finest late medieval English work in this material. It is in **Gloucester Cathedral**, itself the

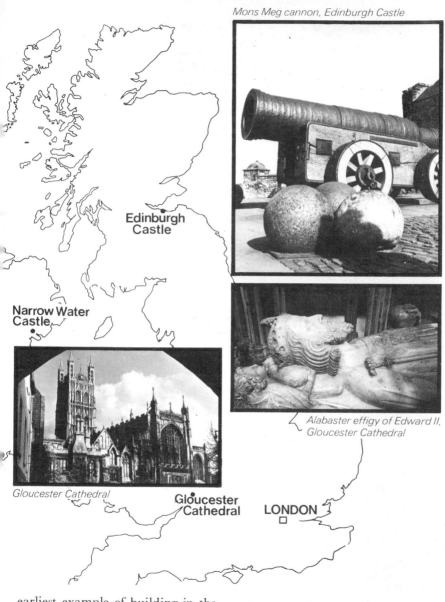

Mons Meg cannon, Edinburgh Castle

Edinburgh Castle

Narrow Water Castle

Gloucester Cathedral

Alabaster effigy of Edward II, Gloucester Cathedral

Gloucester Cathedral

LONDON

earliest example of building in the Perpendicular style.

The Renaissance spirit of adventure found an outlet in the epic sea voyages of the age. This adventurousness was mixed with roughly equal parts of religious zeal, greed for profit, and fanatical nationalism. *Below:* Sir Walter Raleigh, a sixteenth century English explorer

The Renaissance and Reformation

The sixteenth century was an age of new attitudes and energies – so much so that it is often called the beginning of modern times.

In England, the Tudor kings created a strong state, backed by a prosperous middle class that had grown tired of civil war. The rising mood of self-confidence showed itself in splendid country houses, feats of exploration, the epic sea war against Spain, and in the creation of great literature.

The whole of western Europe was shaken by the Protestant Reformation, which split the Christian church into two. England and Scotland eventually became Protestant, but religious questions continued to cause them difficulties both at home and abroad.

The great majority of Irishmen remained faithful to Catholicism. At the end of the century the English managed to re-establish control over most of Ireland, so that native Catholics were ruled by a foreign Protestant power. The conflicts caused by this situation were to dominate Irish history for centuries.

On the death of Queen Elizabeth, the English crown passed to the Scottish king James VI. With the same king on both thrones, 300 years of border warfare ended, and peace seemed within reach for the whole island.

Notable People

Lord Burghley (1520–98). Born William Cecil, chief adviser of Queen Elizabeth.

Sir Francis Drake (died 1596). Most famous Elizabethan seaman and first English navigator to sail round the world. He 'singed the king of Spain's beard' in a raid on Cadiz (1587), and took part in fight against Armada.

Edward VI (1537–53). English boy king 1547–53. Son of Henry VIII. In his reign England became Protestant country.

Queen Elizabeth (1533–1603). Queen of England 1558–1603. Clever and well-served. Introduced a moderate Protestantism. Survived plots and Spanish Armada.

The Earl of Essex (1566–1601). Unstable favourite of Queen Elizabeth, led unsuccessful rebellion; beheaded.

Lady Jane Grey (1537–54). 'Nine days' queen'. Protestant claimant to the crown on death of Henry VIII. Executed by Queen Mary.

Henry VII (1457–1509). King of England 1485–1509. Careful, peaceable, mean: created secure, rich monarchy.

Henry VIII (1491–1547). King of England 1509–47. 'Bluff king Hal', six times married. Needed a divorce from his first wife, Catherine of Aragon, who could not give him a son and heir; the pope's refusal to allow divorce caused Henry to separate English from Roman Catholic church. Other wives: Anne

Boleyn, Jane Seymour, Anne of Cleves, Catherine Howard, Catherine Parr.

John Knox (1505–72). Religious reformer, spearhead of Scottish Protestant Reformation.

Mary I (1516–58). Queen of England 1553–58. 'Bloody Mary'. Brought back Roman Catholicism and burned three hundred Protestants, including Bishops Ridley and Latimer.

Mary, Queen of Scots (1542–87). Quarrelled with her subjects and fled to England in 1568. Became threat to Queen Elizabeth as Catholic next-of-kin; imprisoned and finally beheaded.

Sir Thomas More (1478–1535). Lord Chancellor of England. Opposed Henry VIII's divorce from Catherine of Aragon and break with Papacy; was executed. Catholic saint. Wrote famous book *Utopia* which began the common use of the word to describe an ideal state.

Sir Walter Raleigh (died 1618). English courtier, poet, navigator, coloniser. Failed to found colonies in Virginia, but sometimes credited with introducing potato and tobacco to British Isles.

William Shakespeare (1564–1616). England's greatest poet-playwright. Usually thought of as an 'Elizabethan', although he wrote many works after the Queen's death.

Sir Philip Sidney (1554–86). English poet and soldier, died gallantly in English expedition to help Dutch rebels against Spain.

Thomas Wolsey (died 1530). Cardinal, archbishop of York and chief minister of Henry VIII. Unpopular because of his arrogance and use of his position to make vast fortune.

Fell from power when he failed to obtain king's divorce.

Life during the Renaissance

Population & settlement

The population of England and Wales seems to have increased from about 3,000,000 in 1500 to 4,000,000 at the end of the century. In 1600 there were probably some 800,000 Scots.

A good many Midlands villages disappeared as a result of enclosures. On the other hand, growing demand for fuel led to the clearance of much woodland.

Agriculture & food

There was little change in agricultural methods. Enclosures were much complained of, but seem to have been important only in certain Midland counties.

Early in the sixteenth century, large-scale hop cultivation was introduced into Kent. The technique came from Flanders, as did the distinctively shaped oast-houses used for drying the crop. From the

Americas came the potato, regarded as an eccentric luxury. By contrast, sugar was tremendously popular although also expensive: the Englishman had a sweet tooth (until sugar made it decay), and a wide variety of sweets and cakes were made.

Towns, trade & industry

London went on expanding at a tremendous rate. By 1600 the city had about 300,000 inhabitants. The next biggest towns – Norwich, Bristol, York, Exeter – all had

As evening fell people hurried home. Accidents could occur easily enough in unpaved, unlighted streets, quite apart from the danger of being robbed. The night watch was suspicious of anybody found out of doors without good reason

populations of less than 20,000. The gilds played an essential part in controlling trade, but otherwise there was little public organisation. Streets remained insanitary and unlit, but the larger towns began to employ night watches to keep down crime, drunkenness and disorder.

The sixteenth century was an age of economic growth, but of a rather unsteady kind. In England the cloth trade, for example, experienced some bad times when many weavers were unemployed. Life was complicated (then as now) by inflation, with prices rising steeply over a long period. And enclosures added to the numbers of unemployed, driving a good many people off the land. The number of 'sturdy vagabonds' on the roads was a constant worry for Tudor governments, which devised the first comprehensive system of poor relief to replace the charitable activities of the monasteries. Poor relief became the job of the parishes, so that these church districts became the basic units of local government. In general the gaps between classes seem to have widened, with the middle and upper classes becoming much more prosperous while wage labourers were apparently worse off than in the fifteenth century.

Mining expanded very rapidly – especially mining for coal and iron. English iron artillery was in demand all over Europe, and much woodland was cleared to provide fuel for iron smelting.

Trade contacts were made with Russia, Persia (Iran) and North Africa, and also with Central and South America.

Buildings

This was another great age of building. But whereas large-scale medieval building had been for defence or worship, Tudor building was mainly for comfort or show. Cardinal Wolsey's Hampton Court Palace was taken over by Henry VIII, and royal palaces such as Richmond and Nonsuch were built in the early sixteenth century. But the Crown soon ran out of money. After that it was wealthy and powerful subjects who built 'prodigy houses' – foursquare palatial piles such as Longleat and Hardwick Hall. These owed most to the old perpendicular style, though some elements were adopted from the new and admired Italian Renaissance mode, with arches and columns inspired by ancient Roman buildings.

These larger houses were built of brick or stone. Less wealthy people continued to use local materials – above all wood from the still abundant forests of the South. The most famous type of Tudor house is 'half-timbered' – a framework of wood, filled in with clay, twigs or rubble which was then plastered over; the contrast between dark wooden frame and light plastering gave the house its characteristic look. Half-timbering was older than the Tudor period, but the only reasonably preserved examples, such as Little Moreton Hall, date from then.

Interiors & furniture

The medieval hall survived in the 'prodigy houses' (see Buildings) as a formal reception area, the Great Chamber. The large first-floor room, the Solar, became the Long Gallery, where the whole family could relax and take exercise in bad weather. But in general, houses were designed with more and smaller rooms, allowing greater privacy for individual members of the family.

However, there were still no corridors in houses, which meant that most rooms were liable to invasion by passers-through. The four-poster bed helped to preserve privacy: curtains were attached to a rail at the top, and when they were drawn the bed formed a room within the room. The most celebrated four-poster is the enormous Great Bed of Ware, which must have held so many people that there was more privacy outside than in.

Furniture remained massive and was made to last for generations. Chairs became more common, though children and servants still generally used stools. The first English chairs without arms appeared at the end of the sixteenth century.

For the upper and middle classes life became much more comfortable and convenient – beds softer, chimneys more efficient, glass

Elizabethan furniture was heavy and built to last. Oak was popular and was used for this carved armchair, canopied bed and kitchen table

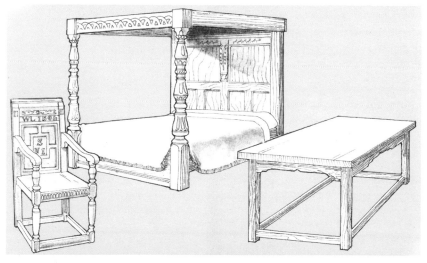

widely used. Those who could not afford sheets of glass could still have lattice windows, consisting of small pieces linked by strips of wood.

But houses remained unhygienic. Rushes stayed on the floors for months and there were no bathrooms. One of Queen Elizabeth's courtiers, Sir John Harington, devised a flush lavatory, but although the Queen installed one, the idea failed to catch on.

Clothing & appearance

In the early Tudor period men wore massively padded doublets that gave them a burly, top-heavy look. Women wore quieter, long gowns and pointed hoods.

In the mid-sixteenth century there were dramatic changes. In particular, men and women began to wear large cartwheel collars called ruffs. These were made up of a mass of gathers and pleats, held in place by wires and later by starch. By the 1590s ruffs had become enormous – as much as 23 centimetres from neck to rim – and in order to eat the wearer had to use a special long spoon. Women's ruffs were often open revealingly at the front.

Rigidity was the keynote of sixteenth century clothing. A person who wore a ruff had to hold up his chin in real or pretended arrogance. Men's doublets were padded and stiffened, and this developed into the strange, hard, curving 'peascod belly' bulging out at the front. Their breeches were also padded. Women wore corsets, and also a 'stomacher' stiffened with wooden ribs, to achieve almost geometrically straight lines tapering to the waist. Below the waist they ballooned out, the result of the extraordinary farthingale – a cage of wire or wooden hoops over which the skirt was draped. Headgear changed notably: stiff, high-crowned, brimmed hats came in for men, and little caps for women.

One of the most luxurious novelties of this luxurious age was silk stockings, which Queen Elizabeth wore from 1561. Only the very rich could afford them: in 1576 a pair cost twenty-five shillings (£1·25), while a pound of butter cost fourpence.

Make-up was used by both men and women. Wigs were often worn: as Mary Queen of Scots' head rolled off the block, her red wig came away.

Tobacco was introduced from America, and pipe-smoking became quite common as early as the 1570s.

Social system

Basically unchanged. Great lords remained locally as well as nationally powerful, though now as servants rather than rivals of the Crown. The gentry increased in numbers and importance. The word 'gentleman' began to take on a new meaning. A gentleman did not necessarily own land, but in order

Serving woman fitting a farthingale to a lady's dress. Farthingales were worn to swell out the embroidered skirts. The purse suspended from the lady's waist held keys. *Below:* The Danny Jewel — a typical piece of Elizabethan jewellery (VICTORIA AND ALBERT MUSEUM, LONDON)

to be accepted he had to show some combination of breeding, education and wealth. In practice, successful men such as lawyers and merchants tended to buy land and retire, thus establishing themselves as country gentlemen. This tradition remained strong until at least the eighteenth century.

Government & justice

The Tudors made the Crown strong again. Many of the old nobility had been wiped out in the civil wars, and their estates taken over by the Crown. War-weariness made many people ready to support the Tudors at all costs; fear of new civil wars encouraged obedience. Many of Henry VIII's actions may look like those of a tyrant, but in fact the Tudors generally made sure that their policies were popular – not so much with the masses, who had no political force, as with the wealthy and propertied. Henry VIII's Re-formation, for example, took advantage of the unpopularity of the church (see Later Middle Ages: Religion) and by selling monastic lands he created a whole class of people with a money interest in supporting what he had done. (See Religion)

Henry also used Parliament to put through the Acts that separated England from the Church of Rome. This recognised Parliament's special role in lawmaking and also strengthened it. By Queen Elizabeth's reign, the Crown was short of money, and forced to appeal frequently to Parliament for subsidies on taxes. Taxation was considered an abnormal procedure – mainly a wartime measure – since the monarch was supposed to live off the income from his lands. When rising prices and other difficulties made this impossible, the monarch had to ask for subsidies more often, which meant that Parliament tended to meet more often and became conscious of greater power.

The House of Commons began to discuss popular grievances and to ask for action before they would vote subsidies. Queen Elizabeth was wise enough to avoid a head-on clash, but Parliament's ability to 'blackmail' the Crown posed a serious threat to future traditional royal rights.

Easily the most important local government officer was the justice of the peace, whose range of duties was widened still further. In effect,

Medal with Henry VIII shown as head of the English Church

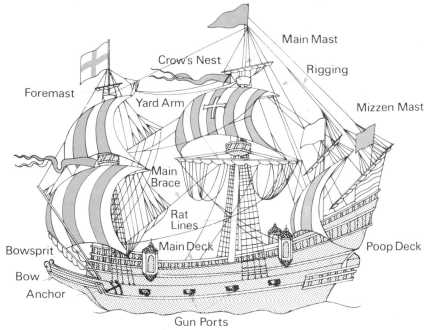

Foremast

Crow's Nest

Main Mast

Rigging

Yard Arm

Mizzen Mast

Main Brace

Rat Lines

Bowsprit

Main Deck

Poop Deck

Bow

Anchor

Gun Ports

British galleons like this were sent out against the Spanish Armada

local government was run by the gentry and in their interests. In practice, royal orders that the gentry disliked were ignored; in Lancashire, for example, where many of the gentry were Catholics, the laws against Catholics were not enforced over wide areas.

In England, Common Law (built up through precedents) remained more important than Civil Law (based on Roman codes and abstract principles). In this, England differed from Scotland and the rest of Europe.

War & defence

There was still no permanent royal

army and in the early Tudor period rebellions had to be put down by foreign mercenaries. Equipment was only modernised in Queen Elizabeth's time, when English troops were raised to help the Dutch rebels against Spain.

Guns were increasingly important, but too expensive to be completely dominant. The English bills and bows gave way to pikes, halberds, small arms (muskets etc.) and artillery. In the new conditions, part armour, such as breastplates, was worn, giving greater mobility.

Henry VIII ordered the building of a chain of coastal forts. He also created the Royal Navy as a permanent force, though battle-fleets

Above: The English, with the better designed ships and guns, defeated the Spanish. *Right:* Course of the Spanish Armada

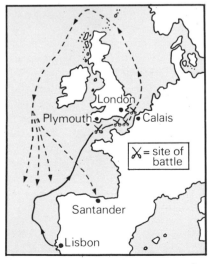

= site of battle

and their crews were still largely recruited from merchant shipping. New dockyards were built, and the galley, with its lines of rowers, was replaced by the ocean-going galleon. The English fleet became the best in Europe. Its superiority over Spain was based on better designed ships with long-range guns (culverins), and also on better seamanship. This was learned in the long semi-official pirate war that went on before the official war with Spain began in 1587. The Spanish Armada, intended as an invasion force, was defeated in battle and suffered even more from appalling weather as it fled round the British Isles; many ships were wrecked on the west coast of Ireland. The war at sea dragged on for the rest of the century, without much offensive success on either side.

Religion

The Reformation meant a change in Christian doctrine, and also a change in appearances and behaviour. Churches became far plainer places: wall paintings were whitewashed over, rood screens and carvings were broken, church plate and gorgeous vestments were sold. The cult of the saints and of the Virgin was swept away, along with indulgences and other practices. Services became simpler and were conducted in English. The wealth and power of the church declined sharply. Monasteries and chantries were dissolved, and the sale of monastery lands enriched the gentry. As their names often make clear, many famous country houses, such as Newstead Abbey, were once monastic dwellings.

The number of clergy was drastically reduced, but on the whole they became better educated. By the late sixteenth century it was becoming common for priests to take a university degree. They were

Newstead Abbey, Nottinghamshire, was a monastic dwelling until the dissolution of the monasteries, when it was sold and became a country house

allowed to marry, and most of them did so.

Churchgoing became a different kind of experience for ordinary people when the solemn rituals in Latin – a language they could not understand – were replaced by services in English. Translations of the Bible created a widespread habit of family readings and prayers at home. The new popularity of sermons showed that, for better or worse, a different kind of religious feeling was developing.

The Reformation created the first really substantial religious minorities since Saxon times. Neither Protestants nor Catholics believed in tolerance, though under Queen Elizabeth it was mainly priests who were executed, since they were regarded as foreign agents. Ordinary Catholics were heavily fined and could not hold public office, with the result that for 250 years they played only a small part in English life. At the other extreme were Puritans – Protestants who wanted to make still more changes. In England these included Presbyterians, who wanted a church organised without bishops and archbishops – which was what eventually happened in Scotland.

Communications

Roads remained primitive. In spite of this, some use began to be made of coaches – which were unsprung, and must have been excruciatingly uncomfortable on the bumpy, rutted surfaces. Communicating by writing became easier because government messengers began to carry private letters. The messengers travelled quickly by taking fresh horses at the special posts set up every few miles along the main routes; from this come expressions such as 'post haste' and 'post office'. Other travellers hired the post horses at each stage, or from inn to inn, rather than wear out their own beasts over the whole of a long journey in bad conditions.

Education

Chantry and other English church

A painting of Trinity College, Dublin, the first Irish university, as it was in the eighteenth century (NATIONAL GALLERY OF IRELAND)

schools disappeared during the Reformation. But the gap was filled in Queen Elizabeth's reign, when there was a great surge forward in education. Both royal and private patrons founded new grammar schools, including such famous ones as St Paul's (under Henry VIII), Harrow, Rugby and Repton. Repton was set up in a twelfth century priory which still forms part of the school buildings. There were about 360 grammar schools in England – probably more per head of the population than existed again until the twentieth century.

The universities of Oxford and Cambridge and the Inns of Court also flourished. Patrons were generous with scholarships and many poor students were able to attend school and college.

The first Irish university – Trinity College, Dublin – was founded. It was, of course, for the English-speaking Protestant minority.

Before going to school, boys learned to read and write. So did many girls but they did not go on to grammar school. Most schools were run by only two teachers, the master and his assistant, the usher. Boys worked about ten hours a day, studying mainly Latin, which remained essential for a career in the law, the church, medicine and government.

Art & ornament

The early Tudor kings imported foreign painters and sculptors who had been trained in the Renaissance style, with its greater realism and emphasis on human dignity. Examples are the German painter Holbein and the Italian sculptor Torrigiani, who carved the tomb of Henry VII in Westminster Abbey. They had no English successors, and Elizabethan art was not particularly distinguished. The exceptions were painters of miniature portraits, which became fashionable on lockets worn round the neck. The miniatures painted by Nicholas Hilliard are brilliant and rather romantically mysterious. Ornament was profuse – often unpleasantly so, as though the artist could not bear the smallest plain area. But much fine woodcarving was done.

Portrait miniature by Nicholas Hilliard

89

Globe Theatre, London, with cutaway to show apron stage, curtained rear stage and balcony

Leisure

Drama in the modern sense developed, and the first professional theatres were built. The old religious mystery and morality plays were replaced by tragedies and comedies. Plays were immensely popular. They were performed by schoolboys, at the Inns of Court, and by companies of actors. These 'players' were not considered really respectable; in fact they were liable to be thrown into jail as vagabonds unless they belonged to a company patronised by a great lord. When not working directly for him, they toured – and it was one of these companies, on tour at Stratford, that probably employed the young Shakespeare. The first theatre was built in 1576 at Shoreditch in London. But London's aldermen were puritans who disliked plays, and from the 1590s theatres were set up across the Thames in Southwark, outside the city boundaries. Shakespeare acted and wrote for the Globe, the most famous theatre of all.

In form the Elizabethan theatre was a balconied wooden O, open to the sky. In the centre was a kind of house from which the 'apron' stage thrust out into the 'groundlings', who paid a penny each to stand round and watch. Above, in the balcony, sat the wealthier patrons. Behind the stage was a dressing room, and above it a separate balcony, also used during the performance.

Two games, bowls and tennis, are particularly known from this period, though they are first heard of in the Middle Ages. Tennis was not the modern 'lawn tennis' game, but 'real' or 'royal' tennis; Henry VIII's tennis court at Hampton Court is the oldest in the world.

Morris dancing was also not new, though from this period began its traditional connection with Maytime ceremonies. Music-making was not just for professionals, but was universally popular. Most educated people were expected to be able to take part in singing a round, and the lute and virginals were widely played.

Royal or 'real' tennis, played indoors, was a pastime of courtiers

History on view

Three royal chapels built by Henry VII are masterpieces of late Perpendicular Gothic, and belong in spirit to the later Middle Ages: **King's College, Cambridge; St George's, Windsor;** and at **Westminster Abbey,** Henry VII's chapel, which also holds the Torrigiani tomb.

Holyrood House

Wollaton Hall, Nottinghamshire

Hardwick Hall, Derbyshire

Hardwick Hall

Little Moreton Hall •

• Wollaton Hall

Repton School
• Kirby Hall

Stratford-on-Avon • Cambridge

Windsor LONDON

Hampton Court

*Anne Hathaway's Cottage,
Stratford-on-Avon*

Longleat

Hampton Court is in Middlesex, just outside London. **Longleat** is in Wiltshire, **Hardwick** in Derby-

Little Moreton Hall, Astbury, Cheshire

shire. Some others are **Holyrood-house** (royal palace), Edinburgh; **Kirby Hall,** Northamptonshire and a wing of **Wollaton Hall,** Nottinghamshire. **Little Moreton Hall** is at Astbury, Cheshire, and several well-kept houses linked with Shakespeare can be seen at **Stratford-on-Avon** in Warwickshire.

There are good examples of interiors at the **Geffrye Museum,** London and the **Victoria and Albert Museum,** London (part of the interior of **Sizergh Castle,** Cumbria). **The Great Bed of Ware** is in the Victoria and Albert, which also has fine collections of musical instruments and miniatures.

The most direct link with the Tudor army is the **Yeomen of the Guard.** This body was created just after the battle of Bosworth, and still exists as the Queen's bodyguard. The similarly-uniformed Yeomen Wardens of the Tower (of London) date from 1509.

Repton School is in Derbyshire.

Great Bed of Ware at Victoria and Albert Museum

St George's Chapel, Windsor

93

The Seventeenth Century

The struggle between king and parliament was the central event of this period. It flared up into civil wars in the 1640s, leading to the execution of the king, Charles I, and the declaration of a republic, the Commonwealth. After a period of semi-military rule under Cromwell, the monarchy was restored in 1660, but stability came only in 1689, when a new political settlement gave Parliament a far greater role in government.

One result of the 1689 dynastic crisis was that James II and his Catholic descendants were exiled. They became a rival dynasty, with a good many supporters (Jacobites), especially in Scotland and Ireland.

Another result was the emergence of Nonconformists – Protestants of various groups who refused to belong to the Church of England. Almost everywhere in the British Isles there were now several rival Christian groups.

Religious hatreds were fiercest of all in Ireland. These, along with the Protestant settlements and a bloody history of massacres and battles, created a bitterness that has existed in some form ever since.

Though sharing the same king as England, Scotland retained a separate government, church and laws. In the civil wars, Scotland played an independent role, siding first with Parliament and later with the king – until she was defeated and occupied by Cromwell's army. Full union between the two countries came only at the end of the period.

The execution of Charles I at Whitehall in 1649 committed England to a puritanical republicanism which was maintained by force until 1660, when the monarchy was restored

In the later seventeenth century England became an increasingly important trading country, laying the basis for future expansion. This tendency carried on even after she joined the European coalition against Louis XIV of France, and became involved in wars that lasted almost twenty years.

The poor had little share in the improvements of the age. Many of those who could, emigrated to the colonies being set up in the West Indies and North America.

95

Notable People

Charles I (1600–49). King of Great Britain 1625–49. Defeated in civil

war with Parliament and eventually executed.

Charles II (1630–85). King of Great Britain 1660–85, after the 1660 'Restoration' ended his exile. Famous for love of pleasure, but

shrewd enough to ride out the storms of his reign and leave a strong monarchy.

Oliver Cromwell (1599–1658). English religious and political leader, emerged as brilliant general of the parliamentary army and ruled England and Scotland

1653–58 as Lord Protector.

George Fox (1624–91). English founder of the Society of Friends ('Quakers').

John Hampden (1594–1643). English parliamentary leader famous for refusal to pay ship money, on grounds that tax was illegal. Killed in civil war.

William Harvey (1578–1657). English physician, discovered circulation of the blood.

James I and VI (1566–1625). King of Scotland 1567–1625 and of England 1603–25. A shrewd survivor, though a far from inspiring personality. Had considerable difficulties with his Scottish nobles and English parliaments.

James II (1633–1701). King of Great Britain 1685–88; younger brother of Charles II. A convert to Catholicism, he was overthrown because of pro-Catholic policies. Fled abroad, then invaded Ireland, but was defeated at the battle of the Boyne.

John Milton (1608–74). English poet who wrote the epic poem

Paradise Lost. Also Latin Secretary to Cromwell.

Sir Isaac Newton (1642–1727). English scientist and mathematician, discovered theory of gravitation and constructed model of the

universe unchallenged until twentieth century.

John Pym (1584–1643). English parliamentary leader, chief organiser of opposition to Charles I.

Samuel Pepys (1633–1703). English civil servant. He was an outstanding secretary of the admirality, but was most famous for

his diary which was fascinating as a personal and historical document.

William (1650–1702) and **Mary** (daughter of James II) (1662–94). Ruled jointly 1689–94; then William, a Dutch prince of the house of Orange, ruled alone to 1702. William led Britain into the long wars with France (1689–97; 1701–13).

Sir Christopher Wren (1632–1723). English architect of genius, designer of St. Paul's Cathedral, London, as well as numerous other buildings throughout the country.

Life in the Seventeenth Century

Population & settlement

By 1707 there were perhaps 5,500,000 Englishmen and 1,000,000 Scots.

The most dramatic population rise was in Ireland, which reached about 2,000,000 inhabitants. A great deal of woodland was cleared to make land available to support the increased numbers. A good many of these were Scots and English settlers brought into Ireland under James I. This was an act of deliberate policy, done to create a loyal Protestant population.

The most densely settled part was Ulster, which had been the most unruly province. (The Protestant majority still exists today, and the present conflicts in Northern Ireland stem directly from Protestant-Catholic hostility.) Catholic Irish support for Charles I, and later for James II, led to heavy confiscations of Catholic lands, so that the Protestant minority became the dominant landowning class right down to the late nineteenth century.

Woodland clearance also went on steadily in England, and in the later seventeenth century a serious effort was made to drain the fens, which in those days covered large areas of East Anglia.

Agriculture & food

In England, enclosures went on steadily, both of settled land and newly cleared woods and fens. Food production increased, most dramatically in Ireland, which exported sheep, wool, cattle and dairy foods. Despite occasional shortages and

bad harvests, agricultural surpluses made famine unlikely; the last serious example took place in Scotland in the 1690s.

Towns, trade & industry

London continued to grow much faster than any other British town, and soon had a population of over 500,000. Even the catastrophes of 1665–6 (the Plague and the Great Fire) had no long-term effect: the destroyed City houses were quickly rebuilt – in brick instead of wood – but unfortunately on the old medieval plan, with narrow, winding, close-packed streets in spite of a modern plan submitted by Wren. The Thames drew in more and more trade, preventing the expansion of the east-coast towns. These also suffered from the development of transatlantic trade, which favoured Bristol and other western ports.

Busy London docks in the later part of the century. Trade and shipping were to become even more important in British life, creating the conditions in which an industrial revolution could eventually occur

Coal and iron production boomed. Ironworking in Birmingham and the black country developed so rapidly that the Warwickshire forests disappeared. In many areas coal started to be used as fuel in the home. Life must have been very hard for people unlucky enough to live in deforested areas that were also far from the waterways on which coal could be transported.

By the 1660s Britain was a bustling trading nation, with the old cloth industry still producing her major export. The techniques and organisations needed to handle complicated financial operations also began to develop. Chief among these was banking. The Bank of England was founded in 1694.

Under Charles II the first proper machinery for making coins was introduced. Designs became more elaborate and the first coins with milled edges appeared. The sovereign was replaced by a new gold coin, the guinea. When currency was in short supply, traders sometimes issued their own tokens.

Scottish prosperity grew more slowly. Under Charles II and William III Scotland was involved in wars on England's side, though this disrupted her trade with Holland and France. Inevitably, Anglo-Scottish trade increased. As the weaker of the two, Scotland suffered from the existence of customs barriers – a strong incentive for her eventual agreement to full political union with England.

Buildings

The 'prodigy houses' continued into the reign of James I. The most notable survivor is Hatfield House, built for the king's chief minister, Sir Robert Cecil. This is a grand, impressive pile, still English/Gothic in style despite a porch with a few classical columns.

The true Renaissance style – with its clean-cut lines, columns, round arches, domes and triangular pediments, – was introduced under Charles I. The earliest examples, built by the architect-designer Inigo Jones, are the neat little Queen's House at Greenwich and the imposing Banqueting House in London.

There was little major building during the Commonwealth, but after the Restoration one of the great ages of English architecture began. The Baroque, a grandiose version of the Italian Renaissance style was followed, though English architects modified the great sweep-

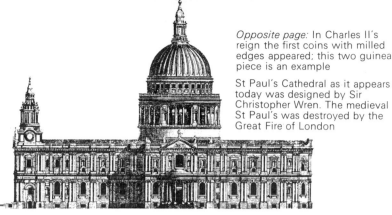

St Paul's Cathedral as it appears today was designed by Sir Christopher Wren. The medieval St Paul's was destroyed by the Great Fire of London

ing curves favoured by the Italians. St Paul's Cathedral is in this style built by the great Sir Christopher Wren to replace medieval St Paul's, destroyed in the Great Fire of London. Wren rebuilt fifty-one of the destroyed City churches, while the citizens were responsible for rebuilding their own houses – in brick this time, not wood.

The opulence of the upper classes is shown by the country houses they built from this time onwards. Often, these were in palaces, for example, Chatsworth, built for the Duke of Devonshire.

Interiors & furniture

In England improvements continued, though not for the poor. Furniture remained basic until after the Restoration. Then, impressed by the sophistication of France, wealthy Englishmen began to acquire veneered, inlaid and lacquered pieces, many of them new to England, for example bureaus and cabinets. In Scotland, the gentry and middle class began to achieve the moderate comforts common in England – houses divided into several rooms, beds, pewter tableware and so on.

Clothing & appearance

Dress was rather more sober than in the previous period, and much less rigid-looking. 'Elizabethan' styles carried on until around 1625. During this time the ruff developed into a stiff thin upright circle; then it was turned down to make a kind of lace collar which at times spread right across the shoulders. Doublets became softer. Bulging trunk hose was replaced by trouser-like garments – knee-breeches, or long Spanish hose worn tucked into high boots. Men wore their hair long, and pointed beards became fashionable. Hats were wide-brimmed. Both sexes wore high heels. The farthingale disappeared from women's dress. Bodices became less

This painting by William Dobson (TATE GALLERY shows the long hair and flamboyant clothes, typical of the time

geometrically rigid, though waistlines were high.

There was little difference in dress between 'cavaliers' and 'roundheads', though puritans disapproved of the more extravagant styles – especially those of the court after the Restoration. Outside the court, men began to adopt less romantic and dashing styles in the later seventeenth century. A coat and waistcoat were worn above knee-breeches, stockings and shoes. They wore wigs and were clean-shaven.

In Scotland, the kilt, and other elements of 'traditional' Highland dress, developed into the form they have always taken since.

Social system

The English social system was shaken up, but not destroyed, during the Commonwealth. Army rule gave influence to men of military ability or religious conviction, rather than property, and some small groups, such as the Levellers and Diggers, visualised a more just and equal society. But with the Restoration the old order returned.

The gap between the comfortably-off and the poor seems to have have continued to widen. Nobility, gentry and yeomanry benefited from the growing wealth of the country, whereas perhaps a quarter of the population had only just enough to survive; at least some of the time such people had to be supported by poor relief.

Class feeling remained strong and was backed up by religion. Before 1660 there were many puritans among the propertied classes; after the Restoration the gentry were mostly firm Anglicans, though Nonconformism strongly attracted the hard-working. independent-minded yeoman. The Game Law of 1671 was a particularly blatant piece of class legislation, making it illegal for a man to kill grouse and other game *even on his own land:* only large landowners could do so.

Merchants improved their status, as trade became recognised as an important source of English wealth. Professional men – lawyers, doctors, clergymen, teachers – emerged as distinct groups with their own standards and interests. Most gentlemen were prepared to see their younger sons enter trade or the professions, so that the social system – though still organised to favour the wealthy – remained fluid.

Government & justice

The struggle between king and parliament was complicated by religion, but the political issue was clear: did royal policy need parliamentary approval? By tradition, Acts of Parliament had a special authority, but parliament itself was not a full-time body: the king summoned a parliament only when he wanted or needed to.

Yet it was parliament that won. The weakness of the king's position was lack of money, which forced him to call parliament frequently and ask for grants of new taxes. (Even in Queen Elizabeth's time, inflation and the increased cost of fighting wars made it impossible for the crown to live on its traditional income.) Parliament would refuse unless they first obtained 'redress of grievance' – the policies or laws they favoured.

The outcome of the struggle, after the Revolutionary Settlement of 1689–90, was that parliament became an essential part of govern-

A contemporary print of Charles I and Parliament

ment. The king kept very considerable powers, but he needed the co-operation of parliament even to keep an army in being. With the growing spirit of tolerance in religion, there were fewer reasons for conflict between crown and parliament, and the two were brought together by the common struggle against France.

Parliament was at this time in no sense a democratic body. Only a small number of people with property could vote in elections to the House of Commons, and often the voters were controlled by local nobles or landlords. For many seats there was only a single candidate, and if a contest did take place it was simply between rival magnates. The result usually did show the mood of the country – the only part of the country that was thought to matter: the property-owning classes.

The 1707 Union between England and Scotland meant that the independent Scottish Parliament ceased to exist. Instead, Scotland sent MPs to the British (formerly English) parliament at Westminster. Laws passed at Westminster were now binding on both countries, though the Scots kept their own legal and religious systems.

War & defence

Before the civil war parliament feared that a large, well-equipped royal army might be used against them. In the event it was parliament's own army that established despotism – though against the will of parliament. This was Oliver Cromwell's New Model Army or Ironsides – tough, well-disciplined, religiously convinced troops, probably the finest army in Europe.

Oliver Cromwell's New Model Army was well-disciplined and probably the finest in Europe

The New Model was disbanded at the Restoration – except for a foot regiment, the Coldstream Guards. This, with two new regiments of life guards, became the nucleus of the first English standing (permanent) army. It was certain to survive because the wars with France went on for so long, forcing parliament and people to accept a rapid expansion. But a parliamentary check was kept on the army by legalising it for only a year at a time – which also made sure that kings could not do without parliament for very long.

Although Englishmen were still supposed to practise regularly with the longbow, no serious use was made of it. The pikeman survived longer, since reloading firearms took so long that infantrymen needed to be protected in the meantime. The introduction of the bayonet later in the century made the use of firearms universal.

Religion

Until the Restoration, most puritans belonged to the Church of England, although they wanted to see it 'purified'. After the Restoration, puritans who would not conform were driven from the Church and formed their own churches: they became 'Nonconformists' or 'Dissenters'. So, in addition to Roman Catholics, there were now also Anglicans (members of the Church of England), Presbyterians, Indep-

endents (later called Congregationalists, from their belief that each congregation should decide the form its worship should take), Baptists and Quakers, distinctive for their simple meetings and refusal to fight or swear oaths. The Church of England remained the official or established church in England, Wales and Ireland. In Scotland the ruling body was the Kirk, which after the 1688 Revolution was entirely presbyterian in organisation. So now society was divided into groups with a variety of religious opinions and, the most unusual aspect of the situation, governments came to recognise that they must tolerate them all. Catholics and Nonconformists were not allowed to hold public office (ie to become MPs, JPs, aldermen), and their sons could not go to the universities but open persecution ended.

Communications

Most people still preferred to travel by water rather than road. Towards the end of the century, turnpikes were set up in England. These involved a charge for the use of the road, in an effort to raise money for improvements. In spite of the difficulties, many more people seem to have travelled about, surprisingly often for the pleasure and interest of sightseeing. Wheeled traffic became more common, and the first regular stage coaches began operation. In England, a postal service

Long coach journeys were made from about 1650, though only by the relatively small number of people who had to. Bad roads made travel uncomfortable, and there were other hazards such as coaches overturning and robbery

carried letters fairly efficiently. After the Restoration the first newspapers appeared in London.

Education

By the late seventeenth century, good writers were developing a plain, effective English prose that is still easily understood today. Even works of scholarship were often written in English, though Sir Isaac Newton chose Latin for his *Principia*, which stated the theory of gravity and other discoveries.

Earlier in the century, grammar school foundations (such as Charterhouse) and endowments had taken place even faster than in Tudor times. The civil war had a disruptive effect, and after the Restoration the dissenting schools and academies proved more go-ahead. These were set up by Nonconformists for children who could not go to the Anglican grammar schools and universities. They gave a more modern training than the traditional Latin-based teaching found in older schools, and over the next century a surprising number of distinguished men came from Nonconformist families.

The London Gazette, an early newspaper

1670.

Numb. 432.

The London Gazette.

Published by Authority.

Art & ornament

The most able painters and decorators continued to be foreigners who came to work in Britain, for example

'Two Ladies of the Lake Family' painted by Sir Peter Lely, a Dutch artist who became principal painter to Charles II

the portraitists Van Dyck, Lely and Kneller. Miniatures remained popular.

Ornament was based on the Renaissance tradition. Incredible richness of effect was achieved in royal palaces and the country houses of the nobility, often with the help of specialist decorative artists from abroad. Common were elaborate wall and ceiling paintings, plasterwork and gilding, intricate woodcarving (notably by a Dutch-born master, Grinling Gibbons), tapestries and carpets.

Leisure

Hunting remained popular, and fox-hunting took on its modern 'sporting' form. With the improvement of guns, shooting became an upper-class occupation. Special game laws prevented other people from taking part, though there must have been plenty of poaching.

In the early Stuart period drama was tending to become a court art. Even more popular at court or in aristocratic houses were masques – set-piece entertainments rather than plays, featuring beautiful scenery and costumes, music, dancing and poetry. During the Commonwealth the theatres were shut by the disapproving puritans, but they re-opened at the Restoration. The new theatres were similar to modern ones – roofed-over, with a 'picture-frame' type of stage and women's parts played by women, not boys. The famous Nell Gwynn for example was an actress.

Restoration London also saw the first public operas and concerts, and England produced her first master-composer Henry Purcell.

History on view

Hatfield is in Hertfordshire. The State Rooms contain a superb collection of period portraits. **The Queen's House** is part of the **National Maritime Museum** at Greenwich, south-east of London on the Thames. Nearby is **Greenwich Naval Hospital**, one of the most clean-lined and splendid of

Greenwich Naval Hospital, London

Sir Christopher Wren's designs.

Surviving Wren churches in London include **St Mary-le-Bow; St Bride's; St James's, Piccad-** illy; **St Stephen Walbrook.** Wren also remodelled part of **Hampton Court Palace** in Middlesex, and designed **Chelsea Hospital**, London, and the **Sheldonian Theatre, Oxford.**

Chatsworth is in Derbyshire. In this period a hard white limestone began to be used for the grander buildings in the 'classical' or Renaissance style. This was Portland stone, which became – and remained – the standard material. It was quarried in the area of the **Isle of Portland**, Dorset, where it can be seen today both as quarried blocks and as living rock.

Sheldonian Theatre, Oxford

Church of St Stephen, Walbrook

The houses maintained by the Shakespeare Birthplace Trust at **Stratford** are good examples of early Stuart interiors.

London Museum has a pleasing diorama of the Great Fire of London and much else of interest.

The Cromwell Museum, Huntingdon, was originally the town's grammar school; Cromwell and Samuel Pepys were pupils there.

Chatsworth House, Derbyshire

Church of St Bride, Fleet St, London

Chatsworth House

Huntingdon

•Stratford-on-Avon

Hatfield House

Oxford

Hampton Court• □LONDON

The Isle of Portland

The Battle of Culloden was more like a massacre, since the ill-armed Highlanders had no answer to the firepower of the Government troops

The Eighteenth Century

In 1714 the British throne passed to a German prince, the Elector of Hanover who was distantly related to the Stuarts. Although foreign, the house of Hanover was firmly Protestant, and only some of the Highland clans were ready to come out in force on the side of the exiled Stuarts. There were two rebellions, in 1715 and 1745, to try and restore the Stuart dynasty. In the second rebellion, the '45, the government had a serious fright when Bonnie Prince Charlie's Jacobite army reached Derby before turning back. In the following years the Highlands were finally and ruthlessly tamed after the battle of Culloden in 1746.

Apart from this, the early eighteenth century was a period of stability in society, politics and religion. British wealth and trade was growing steadily. Trade rivalry became one of the main causes of Britain's wars with France, which brought important conquests in North America, the West Indies and India. Badly mistaken policies led to loss of the Thirteen Colonies (the later USA), but Britain's overseas territories were still of great naval and economic importance.

Wealth, trade, empire and a growing population laid the basis for agricultural and industrial revolutions, both of them well under way by the late eighteenth century. The Industrial Revolution is one of the great events of the history of mankind, transforming first life in Britain and later the whole world.

Also during this period, religious enthusiasm revived through the Methodists and other groups. The first humanitarian reformers in the modern sense also appeared, working to end slavery, bad prison conditions and other injustices.

Ireland remained restless under British rule, though the Act of Union brought her directly under the control of the Westminster Parliament. As well as parliamentary opposition to British rule, there were Irish revolutionaries who hoped to imitate the French example.

The French Revolution of 1789 spread ideas of freedom and equality all over Europe, and encouraged British workers to form political groups. When war with France broke out, the British government suppressed such groups and passed a number of severe laws. The war which had started against revolutionary France, continued with hardly a break against Napoleon's imperial regime. It ended only in 1815, with Napoleon's final overthrow at the battle of Waterloo.

The fall of the Bastille, a famous fortress and prison in Paris, during the French Revolution. French revolutionary ideas of Liberty, Fraternity and Equality found some support in England

Notable People

Jane Austen (1775–1817). Major English novelist, famous for *Pride and Prejudice*, etc.

'Bonnie Prince Charlie', Prince Charles Edward Stuart (1720–88). Grandson of James II, son of 'James III', Jacobite claimant to British throne. Led rebellion of 1745, mainly followed by Highland clans. Army reached Derby before forced to turn back. Defeated at Culloden (1746); escaped. Died in exile.

Robert Clive (1725–74). English soldier; went to India as clerk for East India Company; his political and military achievements laid basis for British Indian Empire.

Robert Emmett (1778–1803). Irish nationalist leader. Hanged after failure of 1803 rebellion.

Lord Edward Fitzgerald (1763–98). Irish nationalist and sympathiser with French Revolution.

George I (1660–1727). Elector of Hanover 1698–1727 and first Hanoverian king of Great Britain 1714–27. He spoke no English and left most English affairs to ministers, so increasing their effective power.

George III (1738–1820). King of Great Britain 1760–1820, attempted to revive royal powers that had lapsed earlier in the century; in 1770s effectively directed govern-

ment till discredited by failures in American war. Suffered several attacks of insanity; permanently insane from 1811.

Duke of Marlborough (1650–1722). John Churchill, English soldier, commanded victorious armies in French wars, notably at Blenheim (1704), Ramillies (1706), Oudenarde (1708).

Viscount Horatio Nelson (1758–1805). English admiral, victor of

battles of Nile (1798) and Trafalgar (1805), which ended French invasion threat, but at which he lost his life.

William Pitt the Elder (1708–78). English politician, chief minister during Seven Years' War, architect of British triumphs in the war.

William Pitt the Younger (1759–1806). English politician, son of Pitt the Elder. Prime Minister 1783–1801 and 1804–06.

Wolfe Tone (1763–98). Irish nationalist who accompanied French expedition to Ireland; was captured and committed suicide to avoid execution.

Sir Robert Walpole (1676–1745). English politician, chief minister 1721–42. Maintained stable if inactive government by skilful man-management and bribery. Often regarded as first prime minister in the modern sense.

James Watt (1736–1819). Scottish engineer who devised first really effective steam engines and steam-driven machines.

Duke of Wellington (1769–1852). Irish soldier who led British army in Peninsular War; defeated Napol-

eon at Waterloo. Later important in politics; prime minister 1828–30.

John Wesley (1703–92). English evangelist, founded Methodist movement.

William Wilberforce (1759–1833). Reformer. Evangelical Christian who led anti-slavery struggle. Secured abolition of slave trade in British Empire (1807). Final abolition of slavery (in the Empire) achieved in year of his death.

James Wolfe (1727–59). English soldier, killed while in command at capture of Quebec which gave British control of Canada.

William Wordsworth (1770–1850). English poet whose simple language and feeling for nature revolutionised poetry. With Coleridge, first great English figure of the Romantic movement; followed by Keats, Byron and Shelley.

Life in the Eighteenth Century

Population & settlement

The population rose slowly in the first half of the eighteenth century, and then increased very rapidly. In England and Wales it reached 6,000,000 by about the middle of the century and was 8,872,000 when the first British census was taken in 1801. Within twenty years it was soaring towards the 12,000,000 mark. Apart from London, the great new industrial areas were the most heavily populated: Lancashire, the West Riding of Yorkshire, the Midlands. The population of Scotland rose to 2,600,000, and Ireland's to almost 6,000,000.

These increases occurred despite considerable emigration. Early in the century, Irish Jacobites fled in large numbers to the Continent, and economic discrimination against Catholics kept the flow going. Protestant Irishmen were driven abroad by poverty and population pressure. And, in Scotland, with the disintegration of the semi-feudal clan system, many Highlanders emigrated to Canada.

The Agricultural Revolution in Scotland brought much virgin land under the plough, including newly drained areas. In England, enclosures encouraged a drift from the land to the rapidly growing industrial towns.

Agriculture & food

The eighteenth century witnessed a gradual but decisive 'Agricultural Revolution'. The size of estates tended to grow, which encouraged efficient large-scale farming. A last great wave of enclosures, affecting about half of all cultivated land, completely ended the old open-field system. Frequently waste or common land was enclosed, causing suffering among village populations. Many people left the land and swelled the numbers of city-dwellers. A new system of crop rotation alternated corn with root crops such as turnips; on this system the soil was never exhausted and therefore did not need to lie fallow one year in three. Cattle could be fed on root crops through the winter and did not have to be slaughtered, so fresh meat, milk and cheese became available all the year round. A mechanical seed drill and the first machines were introduced.

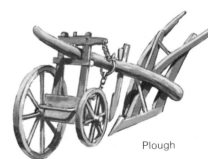

Plough

Flails

Grain

Seed-drill

Butter churn

The 'Agricultural Revolution' was gradual but decisive

Luxuries such as tea and sugar became cheap enough to be enjoyed by most people

In this century the British became confirmed tea-drinkers. Early in the century, coffee-houses were popular social centres for urban dwellers, but tea became so cheap that the mass of the people could afford it. It was drunk heavily sweetened with sugar imported in vast quantities from the West Indies.

Towns, trade & industry

From about the 1780s, the Industrial Revolution began to change the face of Britain. It was solidly based on large (and generally neighbouring) coal and iron fields, rapidly improving communications, already considerable wealth, trade and shipping, rapid population growth which provided both workers and buyers and a highly productive agriculture that could feed the extra mouths. The use of coal (in the form of coke) instead of wood in manufacturing iron led to the tremendous growth of both the coal and iron industries.

The great wool industry became concentrated in the West Riding of Yorkshire. It continued to flourish but was overtaken by the amazing expansion of the Lancashire cotton industry.

Both cotton and wool production

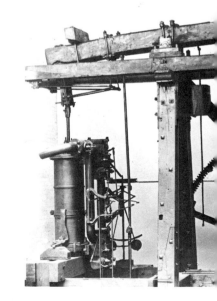

benefited from labour-saving inventions in spinning and weaving, and later from power-driven machinery introduced by Arkwright, Crompton and others. Watt's steam engine, devised to pump water out of mines, was adapted to many kinds of machinery. And when human and animal power were replaced by mechanical power, vast new industrial possibilities appeared.

However, even at the end of the period, the old 'domestic system' (by which most industrial workers did their jobs at home) was only beginning to be replaced by the factory system.

Other important industries included pottery (Josiah Wedgwood established Etruria, his pottery in Staffordshire, in 1760) and in

Boulton and Watts Rotative Steam Engine built in 1788 opened up vast new industrial possibilities (SCIENCE MUSEUM, LONDON). *Above right:* Josiah Wedgwood founded 'Etruria' — the famous Staffordshire pottery factory

Northern Ireland linen became a major industry.

The shift in population centres was reflected in the mushroom growth of certain towns. London remained supreme, with about 1,000,000 inhabitants. But Bristol was being overtaken by Manchester, Liverpool and Birmingham, all rapidly moving towards 100,000. And Leeds, Sheffield and Newcastle were outdistancing older centres such as Norwich. As capital, social centre and port, Dublin's expansion was quite exceptional (it rose to 200,000); Glasgow's was slower, but significant (about 40,000).

The first effective town planning was carried out in this period. There were large-scale developments of terraced squares and crescents for the benefit of wealthy and fashionable city-dwellers These took place in London, Edinburgh and Dublin and also at Bath, which became a great fashionable centre where people socialised while drinking and bathing in the spa waters.

Buildings

These continued to be inspired by the 'classical' tradition of ancient Greece and Rome. But in the eighteenth century it was adapted to give an effect of cool elegance; this style is called Neo-Classical ('New-Classical').

For a time, the older, heavier Baroque style carried on, notably in buildings such as Blenheim, the great palace built for the Duke of Marlborough by Sir John Vanbrugh. But more characteristic were the large number of fine country houses, with their pillared porticoes and low wings stretching away on either side. They still give a strong and immediate feeling of graciousness and civilised comfort. Their gardens and grounds gradually became less formal and more natural-looking, although the effect might well be achieved by 'landscape gardening' – planting, ditching, banking, diverting streams and so on.

Another side of the eighteenth century was a taste for the exotic and picturesque – for sham ruins in the grounds of a house, and for a jokey kind of 'medievalism' and 'Chinese' taste *(Chinoiserie)*. Examples include Horace Walpole's 'Gothick' house (Strawberry Hill) and Kew Pagoda.

In several cities, the first large-scale planned building developments were carried out. By contrast, in the new industrial towns, working-class housing often consisted of row after row of back-to-back houses: ugly, cramped, and so 'jerry-built' that they became hovels within a few years, although they were not necessarily any worse than the shacks in the country that most town workers had recently left behind.

Ugly, cramped back-to-back houses of the new industrial towns sharply contrasted with the other, more exotic, side of the eighteenth century building illustrated by the Royal Pavilion at Brighton (above)

Interiors & furniture

This was the first age that combined elegance with luxury. At first interiors were richly decorated. Later, rooms were designed in the Neo-Classical style associated with the Scottish architect Robert Adam. This was an apparently straightforward style based on simple geometry, but enriched with gilding, ornate plasterwork, panelling, and decorative paintings on walls and ceilings. Fabrics were also used on walls, but a cheaper material was increasingly substituted – wallpaper, made in England or imported from China.

Furniture was made in a great variety of models and types. Here, too, the eighteenth century was the

Left: A Neo-Classical interior. By the late 18th century, interior design had become recognised as an art in its own right. Robert Adam and other experts designed rooms that were opulent but also light and spacious, with elegant furniture, wallpaper, gilding, and plasterwork with abundant mouldings. *Right:* This ornate table with cabriole legs and rich ornamentation is typical of the age

classic age – the age of Chippendale, Hepplewhite and Sheraton, renowned for mahogany masterpieces of veneering, inlay and marquetry. One of the characteristic features was the 'cabriole' leg. 'Chinese' pieces were lacquered, and other features of interior decoration were also designed as *chinoiseries* – sometimes with grotesque or extravagant effects.

Porcelain tableware was widely used and little porcelain figures were popular knick-knacks and table decorations. (Until the early eighteenth century Europeans had not known how to manufacture porcelain, a secret jealously guarded by the Chinese.) Other ceramic ware included items with Neo-Classical reliefs in jasperware, invented by Josiah Wedgwood, founder of the famous Staffordshire firm. Brass fittings, candelabra, firedogs, mirrors and glassware, screens, silverware and a host of other items were beautifully made in this age of supreme craftsmanship.

Clothing & appearance

Men's clothing varied greatly in fashionable detail, but the main elements hardly changed. Long coats were worn over waistcoats and knee-breeches, with cravats or ribbons at the throat. The more formal, collarless coat was close-fitting but flared at knee-level. The looser, informal coat was collared. Close-fitting tights that reached the ankle appeared in the 1790s, and in the early nineteenth century trousers were adopted for casual wear.

The basic outfit for women was a gown consisting of a tight-laced bodice and an overskirt. The overskirt was cut away at the front to reveal an underskirt or petticoat. Wooden hoops beneath the skirts gave them the fashionable shape of the moment. An extra, triangular piece of material, the stomacher, was worn at the front of the bodice, and was often richly embroidered.

Towards the end of the century there was a revolution in women's costume. Dresses became high-waisted, falling almost straight to the ground. They were made of light materials such as cotton and muslin, which were figure-hugging and often semi-transparent. (They were also cheap, thanks to the Industrial Revolution.) Hair became more natural-looking as high-piled styles gave way to apparently simple arrangements of curls.

Caps were the most popular female headgear; the mob-cap worn at home eventually became as large as a hat. More elaborate creations appeared in the 1780s. Shoe fashions in this period varied almost as much as they have in modern times, and wedges, pointed toes and high heels were all seen.

Social system

Little change. The middle ranks of society – people below the gentry but above the poor – increased in numbers, wealth and influence. This was especially so in towns, where they formed the professional and manufacturing classes. But land-owning remained the key to political power and social prestige, and successful men still tended to buy land and retire from business to become 'gentlemen'.

Government & justice

With the country's growing wealth and greater religious tolerance, tensions between king and parliament gradually disappeared. The early Hanoverian kings generally left political work to their ministers, who therefore became much more

powerful. George III tried to control policy more directly, but his efforts were cut short by his disastrous American policy and later his madness.

Ministers controlled policy and most of the time succeeded in keeping majority support in the House of Commons by a mixture of deals and patronage – giving out

The costume of rich and poor was quite different. Fashion was important to ladies and gentlemen, and there were radical changes in style. The more basic, heavy-duty dress of working people changed hardly at all

jobs in return for support. The jobs might vary from a ministry to a post in customs and excise. In fact the history of eighteenth century society could be written in terms of mutually supporting groups such as families, fighting or trading for every scrap of power or influence they could get. Though party labels were used, they meant little. All the groups and individuals who sought power were 'Whigs' in a general sense. But the Tory Party revived during the French Wars, when only a minority who were sympathetic to the French Revolution remained Whigs.

Elections too were usually decided by deals or influence. With only a handful of exceptions, conflicts only occurred between rival influences. Tenants voted for their landlord's choice, and workers for their employer's: without a secret ballot, they dared not disobey. In the counties, all men with property valued at forty shillings (£2.00) could vote. But borough qualifications varied greatly: in some places all men could vote, in others the town council alone nominated the MP. Changes over the centuries had created ridiculous situations, so that one-time villages like Liverpool could not elect a single MP. And most scandalous of all were the 'pocket' and 'rotten' boroughs, in which all the voters might be controlled by a single man.

These abuses were only ended with the Great Reform Bill of 1832.

Reform was in the air from the 1780s, but was delayed by the backlash against the atrocities of the French Revolution. The 1790s began a period of repression which only ended several decades later.

Irish parliaments were generally obedient to royal control until the late eighteenth century. Their greater independence, and the activities of Irish revolutionists, led to the Act of Union in 1801, pushed through the Irish parliament by massive bribing of the members. The Act made Ireland, like Scotland and Wales, part of Great Britain; she lost her own parliament but sent MPs to the British Parliament at Westminster.

Laws grew more, not less, severe. Transportation to America and Australia was introduced. All this was probably a reaction to the enormous growth of population, which created a crime-rate the old parish-constable system could not cope with. Severity seems not to have worked and by the end of the period reform was in the air.

War & defence

The navy became recognised as the Senior Service, vital for preventing invasion, blockading enemies (usually the French) and seizing enemy territories outside Europe. Britain therefore maintained the biggest navy in the world. Its supremacy was seriously challenged only once, during the War of American In-

The press gang pounced on unattached men to make up the numbers in the Royal Navy. Harsh discipline and bad food, wages and living conditions made voluntary service very unattractive

dependence. It owed much to its officer class, which was unusual in consisting of professionals who had passed examinations. But in peace-time ships were laid up (kept 'on the beach') and their crews were paid off. Recruitment was never easy, since conditions below decks were appalling, pay was poor and the lash was freely used to maintain discipline. When seamen were need-ed, many had to be impressed –

forced into service by the press-gang.

The army never had quite the same prestige, despite the victories of Marlborough and Wellington. Conditions were just as bad for the ordinary soldier as for the sailor, and until 1806 he had to enlist for life.

British troops fighting at Blenheim (1704), the Duke of Marlborough's greatest victory in the French wars. *Above:* Blenheim Palace, Oxfordshire, given to Marlborough by the nation

Understandably, most recruits were runaways, or criminals let out of prison to serve, or paupers sent by a magistrate to save the parish money. Officers were not appointed on merit, but bought their commissions. There were some reforms at the end of the period, notably the abolition of billeting in England and the establishment of a Royal Military College.

Religion

The Church of England remained the dominant national religious organisation, worthy but rather lacking in emotional force. The Nonconformist sects also showed little energy. Both were affected by the spirit of the age, which was 'reasonable' rather than dogmatic.

New forces were set in motion by John Wesley, who travelled the country preaching fervently to huge open-air audiences. Although a member of the Church of England, Wesley was opposed by conservatives in it. Eventually he formed his own organisation, run by lay-preachers, and opened chapels for his followers. In this way the Methodist Church was founded. Its impact was tremendous, especially on the masses of people living in the new industrial towns, whom the Church of England had failed to reach. By the end of the period Methodism was the leading Nonconformist sect, and the most vital religious movement in the country.

John Wesley, founder of the Methodist church, travelled the country preaching to audiences in the open air

Hymn-singing was a leading feature of Methodist services, and many famous hymns were composed by Wesley's brother Charles. The Church of England soon followed suit, led by its Evangelical wing. The Evangelical movement was quite small, but many of its members were distinguished. It had close connections with the humanitarian movements that had begun to appear: William Wilberforce was an Evangelical, and other members had close connections with the Sunday Schools.

Communications

The first great age of transport since Roman times. Roads were improved by the widely adopted turnpike system of charging tolls to pay for their maintenance. Great engineers laid long stretches – notably John Macadam, who invented the surfacing named after him. A nationwide stagecoach service followed, and from 1784 special, very colourful mail coaches carried letters and passengers at express speeds.

There was also better river navigation, and the many new bridges included Thomas Telford's famous bridge across the Menai Strait to Anglesey. But it was the 'canal mania' that gave Britain the transport system she badly needed for carrying coal and other heavy materials. Beginning with the canal built by James Brindley in 1759–61 to take the Duke of Bridgewater's coal from Worsley to Manchester, a network of canals spread over the whole country. They were constructed by gangs of labourers (mainly Irish) called 'navigators' – a word still used in shortened form as 'navvies'.

Steam locomotives had not proved their value by the end of the period, but steamboats were already plying the Irish Channel.

Education

Early in the eighteenth century popular periodicals such as *The Spectator* appeared, describing and displaying polite manners and civilised values. They seem to have had a good deal of influence on behaviour.

The leading English grammar schools became national rather than local in intake, accepting boarders and catering mainly for upper-class boys. In this was Eton, Winchester, Westminster and later Harrow became 'public schools' in the modern

Early drawing of the suspension bridge over the Menai straits designed by Thomas Telford (SCIENCE MUSEUM, LONDON)

Gangs of labourers working on the
Manchester ship canal

sense (exclusive private schools).
But standards were often low. Like
Oxford and Cambridge, these
schools concentrated on Latin and
Greek rather than modern subjects,
and the dissenting academies remained the most progressive schools.

There were new efforts to bring
elementary education to poor children. The Charity Schools, set up
early in the eighteenth century, and
the Sunday School movement of the
1780s, were basically religious, with
the aim of turning out Bible-reading,
respectable servants and workers.

Much was achieved by the Society
for the Promotion of Christian
Knowledge, and in the early nineteenth century by the British and
Foreign Bible Society (Nonconformist) and the National Society
(Church of England).

Art & ornament

As well as Neo-Classical buildings
there were Neo-Classical sculptures
by Flaxman and others, which now
look rather cold and inhuman to
most people. By contrast, painting
was warm and often even sentimen-
tal. Gainsborough's work gives an

idealised image of country gentlemen and their wives and daughters; Reynolds and Romney were distinguished as portraitists, but Hogarth was generally harsher, especially in *The Rake's Progress* and

similar satirical paintings and engravings of the vicious side of eighteenth century life. Later on, William Blake produced coloured engravings reflecting his strange mystical beliefs. (He was also the poet who wrote 'Tyger! Tyger! Burning bright'.)

Early Georgian ornament was often elaborate, and in the mid-eighteenth century there were many eccentric 'Chinese' designs. In the second half of the century ornament was generally restrained, though often given prominence by gilding. Classical and floral ornaments (for example chains of flowers, called swags) were popular.

Leisure

The British remained brutal in their tastes, though by the early nineteenth century there were many who disapproved of traditional sports such as cock-fighting and bull- and bear-baiting. Prize-fighting with bare fists – much bloodier than modern boxing – became very popular. Cricket was widely played in the countryside by all classes. Bowling was underarm, and a bat like a hockey-stick was used. Other civilised pleasures included the theatre, taking the waters at spas, strolling in the pleasure gardens opened around London, and visiting seaside resorts such as Brighthelmstone (modern Brighton), made fashionable by George IV.

Bare-fisted prize-fighting and cricket were both popular sports

History on view

For places and things connected with the Industrial Revolution, see the following chapter.

London examples of eighteenth century building developments are **Regent Street** and the **Regent's Park** area, named after the Prince Regent. Edinburgh's **New Town** is even larger, and Bath's many Georgian buildings include the famous **Royal Crescent.** Dublin is still eighteenth century in layout,

Edinburgh

The Four Courts, Dublin

Holkham Hall, Norfolk

Dublin

Holkham Hall

Blenheim Palace

☐ **LONDON**

Bath

Portsmouth   **Brighton**

Chiswick House, London

owing much to specially appointed Wide Street Commissioners. The city has beautiful squares such as **St Stephen's Green** and **Merrion Square,** and impressive public buildings such as the **Four Courts.**

Blenheim Palace is in Oxfordshire. The appearance of its grounds was created by the great landscape gardener 'Capability' Brown. The many individual houses include some in the London area: **Chiswick House, Syon House, Osterley Park House,** as well as **Holkham Hall** in Norfolk and **Prior Park,** Bath. **Strawberry Hill** is at Twickenham (and viewed only by previous arrangement). The pagoda designed by Sir William Chambers is at **Kew Gardens.** Many of the houses mentioned have examples of *chinoiserie* and other styles in furniture and furnishings; so do the **Wallace Collection** and the **Victoria and Albert Museum,** London, and many others. **Brighton Pavilion,** built for the Prince Regent, is the most exotic item of all.

There is a superb display of costumed figures at the **Museum of Costume** in the **Assembly Rooms,** Bath.

The most interesting relics of the Napoleonic wars are the **Martello towers** along the coast, set up to give early warning of invasion. Nelson's flagship, *The Victory*, can be visited at Portsmouth. **The National Army Museum** in Chelsea, London, has exhibits relating to this and other periods.

Many stretches of canal survive and have been re-opened for enthusiasts and pleasure-trippers. Toll houses can also be seen in a number of places, controlling the entrances and exits of turnpike roads.

HMS *Victory* at Portsmouth

133

The Age of Industrial Revolution

Britain changed more in this period than she had in the previous thousand years. Industry replaced agriculture as the chief source of wealth. Sparsely settled countryside gave way to sprawling, noisy, dirty towns. And horse-drawn vehicles and wooden ships were challenged by engine-driven trains, steamships, automobiles and aeroplanes.

Behind all this activity lay the force of the Industrial Revolution. As the first industrialised country, Britain became a world power, dominating the seas with her fleet and expanding her territories into an empire on which it was said the sun never set.

The British way of life changed to fit the new conditions. The middle-

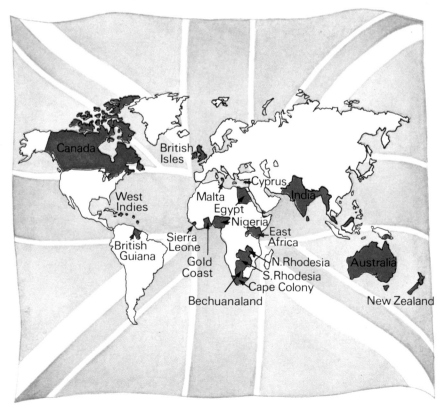

Canada
British Isles
West Indies
Cyprus
Malta
Egypt
India
Sierra Leone
Nigeria
East Africa
British Guiana
Gold Coast
N. Rhodesia
S. Rhodesia
Cape Colony
Australia
Bechuanaland
New Zealand

The British Empire in 1897

During the early Industrial Revolution women and children worked in mines and factories, usually for long periods and in appalling conditions

class code of values came to dominate society. Queen Victoria became the symbol of this, the 'Victorian Age', with its puritan outlook and cult of hard work. Working people had to accept the disciplines of factory life, and gradually organised themselves into political groups and trade unions. In the course of the nineteenth century all men were given the right to vote, and before 1914 women had started to agitate for the same right. The state began to provide a basic education for all, and took the first steps towards looking after people in sickness and old age. Most important of all, although the Industrial Revolution inflicted great suffering on workers, in the long run it led to improvements in their living standards.

There was a geographical shift too. The north of England came into its own as the industrial base of the country, along with lowland Scotland and South Wales. For Ireland the nineteenth century was a sorry story of famine, poverty and mass emigration. The Irish question divided British political parties even after Ireland was finally granted Home Rule (self-government) in 1914. Unfortunately, when war broke out in 1914, Home Rule was shelved.

The First World War marked the end of the prosperous, confident era of British supremacy, and with it came the modern age of great advances, great problems and bewildering changes.

Notable People

Jeremy Bentham (1748–1832). English political thinker whose ideas had great influence during early nineteenth century. Rejected traditional arrangements, arguing that laws could only be judged by their usefulness in securing 'the greatest happiness for the greatest number' (of people). Followers called Utilitarians.

The Brontes, Emily (1818–48), **Charlotte** (1816–55), **Ann** (1820–49). Daughters of a Yorkshire clergyman. Authoresses, individually of *Wuthering Heights*, *Jane Eyre* and *Agnes Grey*.

Charlotte Bronte

Charles Dickens (1812–70). Probably the greatest of the many Victorian novelists. Author of *David Copperfield, Tale of Two Cities* etc.

Benjamin Disraeli (1804–81). English Conservative politician and writer who popularised Imperialism; bought effective control of Suez Canal for Britain. Prime Minister 1874–80.

Michael Faraday (1791–1867). English scientist whose discoveries made possible the practical use of electricity.

George IV (1762–1830). Also called 'the Prince Regent', ruling during George III's insanity. King 1820–30. His fashionable and scan-

dalous life set the upper-class tone for the 'Regency period' (around 1810–37).

William Ewart Gladstone (1809–98). English Liberal politician, great rival of Disraeli. Notable for Irish reforms, but failed to get Home Rule (self-government) for Ireland. Four times Prime Minister.

Keir Hardie (1856–1915). Scottish politician, first Labour Party leader in British parliament.

Daniel O'Connell (1775–1847). Irish leader, 'the Liberator', most successful in 1820s agitation for Catholic emancipation.

Lord Palmerston (1784–1865). 'Pam', English politician remembered for aggressively nationalistic policies. Prime Minister 1855–65.

Emmeline Pankhurst (1858–1928). English leader of the militant suffragettes. Her daughters Sylvia and Christabel were also prominent in the movement.

Charles Stewart Parnell 1846–91). Irish nationalist leader in parliament. United Irish behind him until ruined by scandal.

Sir Robert Peel (1788–1850). English politician, reformed law,

set up police force, founded modern Conservative Party. As Prime Minister (1841–46) repealed Corn Laws and made Britain a free-trade country.

Sir Walter Scott (1771–1832). Scottish poet and novelist, began European fashion for historical novel; great influence on Romantic movement in literature.

Lord Shaftesbury (1801–85). English social reformer, secured first effective Factory Act (1847), making maximum 10-hour working day; also Act forbidding use of climbing boys in chimney-sweeping.

George Stephenson (1781–1848). English engineer who constructed first railway (Stockton and Darlington, 1825) and famous 'Rocket', engine.

Queen Victoria (1819–1901).

Reigned over sixty years (1837–1901). Gave her name to 'Victorian era' characterised by puritism and belief in hard work and general progress.

Life during the Industrial Revolution

Population & settlement

Population increase continued to be dramatic, reaching a total of over 40,000,000, although it was slowing down in the years before 1914.

The increase was all the more striking for being achieved despite some losses. For example, several million British people emigrated (mainly to North America and Australia). And though the Irish population soared to over 8,000,000 by 1841, 1,000,000 died during the famine years 1845–48 and 1,000,000 more emigrated. This set a pattern of emigration and declining population (down to 4,000,000 by 1914).

The only substantial foreign immigration was of Jews from Eastern Europe, fleeing the Russian pogroms (massacres) of the 1880s.

Ireland, inevitably, remained rural and backward. But in Britain there was a major population shift from the countryside to the towns. Long before 1914, Britain had turned into a primarily urban society.

Agriculture & food

In 1815 the landed interest was still so powerful that the Corn Laws were passed, which kept foreign-grown cereals out of the country until the price of British-grown produce became exceptionally high.

The further progress of the Industrial Revolution brought changes. Large numbers of agricultural labourers went to find work in cities and factories; those left behind remained very badly paid all through this period. In 1846 the Corn Laws were abolished to ensure cheap food for the urban masses.

British agriculture enjoyed a 'golden age' from 1850. But in the late 1870s it came to an end with a series of bad harvests and an invasion of cheap wheat and tinned and refrigerated meat from North

Above: The first convenience foods appeared towards the end of the nineteenth century. This can of tripe dates from about 1880. *Right:* Painting of 'The Irish Famine' by G. F. Watts

America, Australasia and Argentina.

In Ireland, living standards fell as population increased without a proportional economic growth. Potatoes now became the staple food, providing basic nourishment – until the great crop failures of the 1840s brought mass starvation and emigration. Conditions afterwards improved, helped by state-aided schemes allowing tenant farmers to buy the land they rented.

For the rest of the country, food was relatively cheap and plentiful, especially in the second half of the nineteenth century. Cheap bread could be covered with a cheap butter-substitute – margarine, introduced in the 1870s. The first generally available convenience foods – tinned, boxed or bottled – appeared.

Towns, trade & industry

In the first half of the nineteenth century, Britain became 'the Workshop of the World'. Her established industries boomed, and a vast new range of engineering goods, machines and other manufactures were made for the home and foreign markets. Financial institutions developed techniques for large-scale operations, such as banks and the Stock Exchange (founded in the 1770s). These were helped by laws that made it easier and safer for people to create and invest in large ('joint-stock') companies with many shareholders. The City of London became the financial centre of the world; Lloyd's, for example, insured trading operations everywhere.

These tremendous achievements largely resulted from uncontrolled private business activity. Understandably, Victorians were suspicious of government interference with what seemed a benevolent freedom. In fact, one of the landmarks of the age was the abolition of government duties on imports and exports. 'Free Trade', established in the 1840s, meant imports of cheap (duty-free) food for the masses and cheap raw materials for industry.

But absolute business freedom also created problems that individuals could not solve and distrust of government interference delayed necessary action. For example, industrialism created hideous, soot-

Print of Lloyd's of London in Victorian times

blackened towns and factories, and even destroyed parts of the countryside. And, even more important, it inflicted enormous suffering on the labouring masses.

Not only men, but also women and children, worked inhumanly long hours in dirty, dangerous conditions. These were only gradually controlled and improved by a series of Factory Acts from 1833. The problem of poverty was still harder to solve. Even people who had jobs often suffered want, and some periods like the 'hungry forties' passed into legend. Militant working-class political activity, such as Chartism, brought no relief. But emigration was a way out, and one taken by millions of people down to the 1880s.

The problem was complicated still further by the 'trade cycle'. Industrial society brought alternating periods of great prosperity (booms) and of collapse (slumps), and nobody knew how to control them. Slumps led to unemployment – and the only form of social security was poor relief. The old parish system failed to cope with the situation, and in 1834 a new Poor Law was passed. Those who needed relief had to come and live in the 'workhouse', where life was made as unpleasant as possible to discourage 'idlers'.

The Poor Law was gradually administered more humanely and, as the century progressed, conditions grew steadily better for a

Life in the workhouse was made unpleasant so as to discourage 'idlers'

majority of ordinary people, who at least began to benefit from industrial progress. They were better fed, better housed and probably led more interesting and leisured lives than before the Industrial Revolution. By the end of the nineteenth century, powerful craft and industrial trade unions existed, and after 1906 Liberal governments brought in the first social security legislation (old age pensions and national insurance). But a surprisingly large proportion of the population remained desperately poor: perhaps 25 per cent at subsistence (bare survival) level – or below it.

The gold sovereign was revived in 1817, replacing the guinea. The first peacetime paper money was issued in 1841, though it could still be cashed at the Bank of England for gold.

Buildings

Industrial building took place on a vast scale. The results were impressively solid and efficient, though often grim-looking even before they became soot-blackened.

Much early Victorian housing for the poor was appalling. But there were also substantial developments with rows of terraced or semi-detached houses for middle-class and upper (skilled or regularly employed) working-class people. Flats became common, especially for the upper-class and the poorest. Transport improvements made it possible for many people to live in city suburbs, which grew rapidly.

Most Victorian building was done bit by bit, with no overall, properly thought-out plan, and often close to factory smoke and grime.

City planning as we know it today lay in the future, but some promising smaller-scale schemes were tried. Port Sunlight and Bournville were 'model' industrial estates set up by benevolent employers. London's Hampstead Garden Suburb was a residential area on the same lines. And in the early twentieth century the first 'garden city', Letchworth, was developed – a spacious separate town, with the right amount of industry to support a limited population, surrounded by a 'green belt'.

There was no new architectural style. The great styles of the past were copied, accurately but often without much judgement. 'Neo-Gothic' was the favourite style, looking rather odd when applied to a railway station or semi-detached, though quite acceptable on the new parish churches. Despite 'Egyptian' mills and 'Byzantine' cathedrals, much public building especially in the 'Classical' style does have a solid dignity.

Port Sunlight, one of the first industrial estates

Interiors & furniture

These showed the effects of the technological revolution. Candles and oil lamps were replaced by electric lighting. Gas cookers and sewing machines were introduced. Furniture and fabrics were first standardised for mass production and later actually made by machinery. Mass-produced goods were often heavy and tastelessly overdecorated, but they were rela-

Above: A Victorian sitting-room crammed with furniture and knick-knacks. *Left:* Toys, such as this doll, were popular

tively cheap and helped thousands of people to create comfortable, respectable homes. To us, the mid-nineteenth century middle-class house would seem hopelessly cluttered – the parlour crammed with furniture, drapes, screens and an unbelievable number of knick-knacks, such as glass-covered stuffed animals, feather pictures, beadwork, shell collections and embroidery. All this reflected the home-centred quality of Victorian life, with its domestic family hobbies and inexpensive servants to do most of the housework. The growing mass of respectable working-class people imitated this life-style as closely as they could.

Clothing & appearance

There was greater variety of costume than ever before, thanks to growing wealth and the appearance of specialised outfits. Until the nineteenth century clothing might be more or less elaborate but unchanged in cut; the only serious exception was riding costume. Now there were clothes for different occasions, occupations, and even times of day. There were morning coats, dinner jackets, smoking jackets, Norfolk jackets worn with knickerbockers; for women, walking dresses, wedding dresses, evening gowns, suits, bicycling outfits, and so on.

The main tendency in ordinary wear was towards a subdued look that suited 'Victorian' ideas of respectability. By the 1840s the frock coat had become standard for men. It was a collared coat that reached knee-level, and was worn over waistcoat and trousers. In the 1870s jackets of the modern type appeared, some as part of lounge suits, though the frock coat did not entirely disappear until the First World War. For a time, hair was worn long, often partly covering the ears, and (apparently) slightly disarrayed. Beards were popular, and so were sidewhiskers – especially in the 1860s, when enormous 'Dundrearies' became fashionable. Soon afterwards a generally neater look was adopted: short hair with

Nineteenth century costumes

A typical Victorian bonnet

1847

and grotesque as the sixteenth century farthingale. And the bustle of the 1880s meant that fashionable ladies moved about with big, artificial behinds in tow.

The change in attitude towards children led to the first clothing styles made especially for them, Eton jackets and sailor suits.

clean-shaven face, or pointed moustaches with or without a spade-shaped beard.

By the 1840s women too were giving up daring and colourful styles. Their bodies were covered by long dark dresses with high necks, and outdoors they wore cloaks and blinker-like bonnets. But extravagances of shape, if not of colour, soon returned. The crinoline, a wire cage worn beneath skirts, attained proportions as enormous

Social system

Ownership of land still gave great prestige, but a substantial, purely town-dwelling upper-middle and middle-class developed. By the later nineteenth century, the greater landed and commercial interests formed an essentially united upper-class whose sons went to the same public schools. From these they emerged as 'gentlemen', now more important than ever as a definition of the upper-class man.

On the land, the trend to large-scale farming squeezed out smaller men, and even at the beginning of the period there were writers lamenting the disappearing 'yeomen of England'. A similar gulf existed in the factory between 'master' and 'man', but in smaller trades and commerce there were many grades and sub-classes – of skilled and semi-skilled, clerks, and so on. The need for records, copies and letters created a large clerical class, 'white-collar workers', and therefore socially superior to men who used their hands, though not necessarily better paid or less hard-driven.

1889   1881

Government & justice

The main features of modern British government were established during this period. It became recognised that kings must choose ministers whom parliament would support, and that the 'advice' of the minister would become royal policy – that in reality ministers would run the country but would be answerable to parliament. The dominant body in parliament was the House of Commons, though the House of Lords remained able to block legislation proposed by the Commons until 1911, when this was limited to two years. A series of Reform Bills made the House of Commons a much more democratic body, elected by secret ballot (1872) by virtually the whole male population. In the years before the First World War, militant women – the suffragettes – began to march and demonstrate to demand the vote. A two-party system emerged: Whigs and Radicals united to form the Liberal Party, while the Tories developed into the Conservatives, though other groups like the Irish Nationalists sometimes interfered with the system. By the end of the period the Labour Party was becoming established as a radical competitor of the Liberals. Government itself became more efficient and honest after examinations were introduced for civil service appointments.

In the Empire, the larger European-settled colonies moved towards self-government. Ironically, Irish Home Rule was bitterly resisted by Conservatives and the House of Lords. Protestant Irish fears were played upon, and Ulster's opposition to Home Rule nearly led to civil war. Home Rule was granted to the Catholic south in 1914, but was never carried out because of the outbreak of the First World War.

During this age of reform, conditions in prisons were greatly improved and the stocks and the pillory were no longer used. Sir Robert Peel founded the first real police force.

War & defence

1815–1914 was an age of peace for Britain. Her only wars were distant ones, and relatively small in scale. The army was small, used mainly for colonial ventures, and neglected: which is one reason why it did badly at the start of the Crimean and Boer Wars and similar crises. However, the worst abuses of army life were remedied after 1870: buying commissions was abolished, flogging ended and shorter (six-year) enlistment was introduced.

The British relied on the navy – by far the biggest and most powerful in the world – to protect them and their empire. German attempts to build a rival battle fleet led to a

Emmeline Pankhurst being 'escorted' from outside Buckingham Palace during a Suffragette rally

A cavalry charge at Balaclava during the Crimean War

naval race which increased international tensions and helped bring about the First World War.

Religion

Catholics and Nonconformists at last gained civil rights through the repeal of the Test Acts in 1828–29. In 1869 the Anglican Church in Ireland was disestablished (lost its privileged official position), ending a situation in which the Catholic majority paid tithes to support the church of the ruling minority.

Distrust of 'popery' (Catholicism) lingered on for at least half-a-century, but otherwise hostility between the various Christian sects died away. The religious revival continued, contributing to the deeply earnest atmosphere of the Victorian age. Piety was domestic and concerned with morals rather than dogma or ritual. An exception was the Oxford Movement of the 1830s, with its stress on the independence of the Church (of England) and on its Catholic elements. This, and later movements in favour of more elaborate ritual, were intensely controversial and unpopular with the majority of churchgoers.

The Church of England recovered much of its energy after a long period of torpor. Pluralism (holding more than one benefice) was abolished, and clergymen were more fairly paid. More bishoprics were created to cope with new centres of population, and – above all – a huge number of new churches were built.

In spite of such efforts, many of

Darwin's theory of evolution suggesting that man and ape had common ancestors outraged many Victorians

the poorest workers had little contact with organised religion. The Salvation Army was founded (1865) to try to reach such people, its bands playing in the streets and its 'soldiers' carrying their message into public houses.

On an intellectual level, all the churches found it hard to cope with geological and biological facts that contradicted the Bible stories – and especially with Charles Darwin's theory of evolution, which made Man himself a descendant of earlier animals. But outright disbelief remained rare even among the educated.

An early Salvation Army Band playing in the streets of London's dockland

Steam truck and trailer

Electric tra

Communications

These improved rapidly. The first railway was opened in 1825, and by mid-century there was a national network. The canals and mail coaches – both at the height of their development – became obsolete. The roads were left free for lighter traffic such as gigs and hansom cabs, threatened, at the end of the period, by the motor car.

For the less well-off, local travel was made easier by horse omnibuses (later motorised). In London, the Underground system was opened, giving Londoners cheap, efficient transport and making it possible for thousands to live in the suburbs and work in the City. In the 1890s bicycle riding became extremely popular, both for pleasure and as a way of ending the isolation of the remoter areas.

Iron replaced wood in ship construction, but steam did not completely replace sail until the introduction of the turbine engine in the early twentieth century. At about the same time, the first successful aeroplanes were built.

Canal barge

Passenger train

Penny farthing

Early Daimler

Goods train

Omnibus

First steamship

Communication without travel was also revolutionised. The penny post (1839) made correspondence convenient and cheap enough for all. The electric telegraph was established shortly afterwards. Newspapers were eagerly read, especially after the appearance of the first determinedly 'popular' paper *(Daily Mail,* 1896), written in sensational style to attract the poorly educated masses. And by the late nineteenth century, the telephone system had started and typewriters were becoming common in offices.

Telephones and typewriters (SCIENCE MUSEUM, LONDON) became common in offices by the end of the century

Education

The state at last intervened to make sure that every child had some sort of education. Elementary education was provided under the Act of 1870, and became compulsory. Religious schools continued to function (as they still do), but where none existed, 'Board Schools' were built and maintained. Secondary education followed in an Act of 1902.

Victorian children of the ruling classes were normally sent as boarders to the public schools. These had been greatly improved in the early nineteenth century by reforming headmasters such as Dr

Victorian schools were strictly disciplined. Most of the work involved reciting and memorizing facts

Art & ornament

Victorian painting and sculpture was often technically skilful but marred by a lifeless sentimentality. However, one school of painters, the Pre-Raphaelites, did produce work that was colourful and intensely romantic yet convincing.

Factory mass-production of goods made them cheaper and more plentiful, but standards of design fell sharply. A wide range of ornament was used – all of it plundered from past styles, and often applied abundantly and tastelessly.

A William Morris design, still popular today

Arnold of Rugby. 'Character training', intensive study of Greek and Latin ('Classics'), and games were their hallmarks. Scientific and technical studies were neglected.

Oxford and Cambridge were little better in this respect. But their higher-educational monopoly was broken by more modern-inclined foundations – individual colleges which eventually developed into universities. London (University College, 1828) and Manchester (Owens College, 1845) were founded. Colleges for women were also set up at Oxford and Cambridge.

Later in the century there was a revival of craftsmanship by William Morris and the Arts and Crafts Movement which did something to improve design as a whole. But the only truly original style was Art Nouveau, which appeared in the 1890s. Its luxuriant, winding lines

A nineteenth century art nouveau poster

suggested climbing flowers and leaves, which often formed a background to such things as serpents and elongated nudes. Art Nouveau was particularly effective on jewellery and household items such as lampstands. But its supreme expression was in the poster, which was transformed by the invention of lithography into a mass-produced art.

Leisure

Early in the period, bull- and bear-baiting and cock-fighting were made illegal. Cock-fighting lingered on in remote areas, while another illegal sport – bare-knuckle prize-fighting – remained popular until the late nineteenth century.

Victorian enjoyment of home life led to an interest in indoor pastimes: charades and other parlour games, singing at the piano or more formal 'musical evenings', stately games of 'ping-pong'. (The dynamic version, table-tennis, is a twentieth century creation.)

In the late nineteenth century, sports such as football and boxing were organised and given standardised rules. The first professional players appeared, but most games were dominated by enthusiastic amateurs.

Melodramas and music-hall (variety) turns were popular, especially in the cities. And by 1914 the earliest silent films and commercial cinemas had appeared.

Above: The music hall was a special kind of variety theatre. Entertaining announcements were made by the chairman, who banged his hammer to compel silence, and the audience took a lively part in the proceedings. *Right:* Silent films appeared during the first years of the twentieth century.

History on view

The mills, factories, stations, bridges and canals of the Victorian era can still be seen in the often densely concentrated older industrial areas. In recent years 'industrial archaeology' has developed as a new study, rescuing and recording the buildings and machinery of the immediate past. Good places to start with are the **North of England Open-Air**

North of England Open-Air Museum, Beamish

Museum at Beamish, Durham, and the **Ironbridge Gorge Museum**, Telford, West Midlands. **The Science Museum,** London, and the **Royal Scottish Museum,** Edinburgh, have collections of nineteenth century machinery, and also models which you can work yourself. The **Gladstone Pottery Museum,** Stoke on Trent, is a splendid group of buildings that has been turned back into a working pottery.

The Victorian slums have vanished. Most old buildings that are now slums were once decent houses, ruined by age and neglect. The heavy 'classical' grandeur of

northern town centres such as Liverpool and Leeds is typically Victorian. **Port Sunlight** (now part of Bebington, Cheshire), **Bournville** and **Letchworth** preserve their original character.

Many blackened nineteenth century industrial townscapes were cleaned up or swept away and replaced by shopping centres or estates in the affluent 1960s; where they survive, it is often on the fringes of big towns such as Leeds. A particularly striking, well-preserved mill town is **Hebden Bridge** in West Yorkshire, which has even become a tourist attraction.

Victorian historical imitations in building are abundant. Grandiose and 'Gothic' in the extreme are **St Pancras** railway station and the **Albert Memorial,** London, and the **Scott Monument,** Edinburgh. **Westminster Cathedral** is 'Byzantine' and the **Ashton Memorial** at Lancaster 'Baroque' – very much Lord Ashton's private version of St Paul's Cathedral.

A wide range of 'Victoriana' can be seen in many antique shops.

Photography was invented in the nineteenth century. It provides abundant direct visual evidence from about the middle of the century. There are occasional exhibitions of such photographs – and many are collected in books available at public libraries.

Gladstone Pottery Museum, Stoke on Trent

St Pancras Station, London

Albert Memorial, London

Edinburgh

Beamish

•**Lancaster**

•**Hebden Bridge**

•**Port Sunlight**

Stoke•**on Trent**

Bourneville•

Letchworth•

□ **LONDON**

Modern Times

The First World War weakened Britain, and the years between the two World Wars were difficult ones. The old major industries declined and there was mass unemployment, at its worst during the world depression of 1929-33.

The southern, mainly Catholic part of Ireland became independent as the Irish Free State, which was eventually declared a republic, breaking all links with the United Kingdom.

Although her policies were uninspiring during the 1930s, Britain played a major role in the defeat of Nazi Germany in the Second World War. For some years after the War she continued to behave like a world power, though in fact she could not hope to compete with the two 'superpowers', the USA and USSR. After the humiliating failure of the Suez expedition against Egypt (1956), more realistic views gradually came to the fore.

During the 'Austerity Period' after the War, a Labour government nationalised several major industries and laid the basis for the Welfare State. From this time, government control or planning became a feature of many areas of British life, regardless of which party was in power.

The 1950s brought 'the Age of Affluence' – a steadily increasing prosperity enjoyed by the great mass of ordinary people. The 1930s had made cinema and radio mass pleasures; in the 1950s, the combination of wealth and technology made available television, cars, refrigerators, vacuum cleaners, washing machines, record players.

Affluence helped to change behaviour – most strikingly, the behaviour of young people, who for the first time had a good deal of money and freedom. In the 1960s youth gave the lead in clothes, 'pop'

Health clinic in the 1950s. Improved nutrition and medical care made the British a far healthier people than they had been before the Second World War

music and much else, but this trend was less marked in the 1970s. The 'media' – communications – had an increasing influence. Cinema and television spread the same ideas and fashions into the most remote areas, and one result was to part-Americanise British culture.

European influences also became strong as the Common Market countries went from strength to strength. The British Empire rapidly dissolved in the 1950s and 1960s, and eventual membership of the Common Market seemed to bind Britain to the Continent more firmly than for centuries.

The 1970s were uncomfortable and less carefree than the previous decade. Tensions in Northern Ireland exploded into violence, and at times terrorists even operated in England. Massive immigration caused social and political tensions. Nationalist trends appeared in Scotland and Wales. And although the standard of living remained high, slow economic growth and rising prices and unemployment checked the progress of the 1960s. In the later 1970s, hopes of future wealth tended to be pinned on the huge quantities of oil and gas found in British waters in the North Sea.

Notable People

Clement Attlee (1883–1967). English politician, prime minister of first Labour government with parliamentary majority (1945–51).

John Logie Baird (1888–1946). Scottish inventor, pioneer of television.

Stanley Baldwin (1867–1947). English politician, Conservative Prime Minister 1923–4, 1924–29, 1935–37.

The Beatles. Outstanding English pop group, dominating period 1963–71. Members: John Lennon (born 1940), Paul McCartney (born 1942), George Harrison (born 1943), Ringo Starr (born 1940).

Neville Chamberlain (1869–1940). English politician, prime minister 1936–40. His policy of 'appeasement' involved attempts to avoid war by satisfying many of Hitler's demands.

Charles Chaplin (1907–77). English film actor and director, created 'Charlie' figure of classic slapstick 'silents'.

Winston Churchill (1874–1965). English politician, inspiring orator who led Britain through Second

World War; Prime Minister 1940–45, 1951–55.

Edward Heath (born 1916). English politician, Conservative prime minister 1969–73.

James Joyce (1882–1941). Irish writer, pioneer of experimental

writing. Author of *Ulysses*.

D. H. Lawrence (1885–1930). English novelist and poet, brilliantly original in style and tone; notorious in own time for open treatment of sexual questions.

David Lloyd-George (1863–1945). Welsh politician, led country in First World War. Prime Minister 1916–22.

Ramsay MacDonald (1866–1937). Scottish politician, leader of Labour Party. Prime Minister 1924, 1929–31, and, as head of mainly Conservative 'National' Government, 1931–35 – for which most Labour Party supporters regarded him as a 'traitor'.

Harold Macmillan (born 1894). Scottish politician, prime minister 1957–63, period when Britain clearly became 'affluent society'.

Field Marshal Bernard Montgomery (1887–1976). Irish soldier, during Second World War, commanded British army in North Africa (won battle of El Alamein, 1942) and Northern France.

Laurence Olivier (Lord Olivier) (born 1907). English actor, recognised as most outstanding actor of

his generation. First of his profession to enter the House of Lords.

Bertrand Russell (1872–1970). English philosopher, writer, political activist. Campaigner against British manufacture of nuclear weapons.

Ernest Rutherford (1871–1937). New Zealand-born British physicist, pioneered research into nuclear fission, leading to both H-bomb and peaceful exploitation of nuclear energy.

George Bernard Shaw (1856–1950). Irish playwright, critic, public personality, combined wit and earnestness in service of socialism and 'creative evolution' philosophy.

Eamon de Valera (1882–1975). Irish politician, bitterly hostile to British. Led republicans who refused to accept 1922 treaty and fought civil war. Later successful politician. Several times Prime Minister and President.

Sir Harold Wilson (born 1916). English politician, Labour Prime Minister 1964–69, 1973–76.

W. B. Yeats (1865–1939). Great Irish poet, wrote in English but associated with revival of Irish national culture.

Life Today

Population & settlement

In the United Kingdom (Great Britain and Northern Ireland) population increased, though more slowly than in the nineteenth century and with periods of little or no growth. In the 1970s it stood at about 56,000,000.

The population of the Irish Republic eventually fell below 3,000,000 and only started to rise in the last few years.

Immigrants from the West Indies, India and Pakistan arrived from the 1950s, mainly settling in the larger cities. Their different colour and customs led to much social tension, and in 1962 an Act drastically limited further immigration. At the time of the 1971 census coloured

Commonwealth immigrants and their families numbered some 1,500,000.

Agriculture & food

British agriculture recovered from the late nineteenth century depression. From the 1930s it was helped by a quota system (limiting imports)

and subsidies (payments to farmers, enabling them to charge lower prices). The work force continued to grow smaller, but production rose impressively with increased mechanisation. In modern times Britain has had one of the most highly mechanised and efficient agricultural industries in the world.

Left: Children from many nations play in the school ground. *Above:* The modern shopping basket. Many items in it come from exotic lands, thanks to swift transport and the deep freezing that preserves them. Machine mass-production methods help to feed millions; scientific controls and checking, help to ensure general health

Ireland remains a primarily agricultural country, with more recent but quite impressive mechanisation.

Affluence, and the development of tinned, frozen and dried products, made most of the world's foods available to ordinary British and Irish people.

Towns, trade & industry

Britain's industrial supremacy had disappeared by 1918, but she remained a wealthy country. Population increased, and cities grew bigger and bigger. In some places, several neighbouring towns expanded until they met and merged in a vast 'conurbation', like Birmingham and surrounding towns – a fact recognised by the setting up of special 'metropolitan counties' in 1974.

This has been a century of difficult adjustments. Older industries such as shipbuilding and cotton went into a long slow decline, creating semi-permanent 'Depressed Areas'. Unemployment was high between the wars, rising to over 3,000,000 at the height of the Depression. Industrial workers had already suffered a bad defeat in the General Strike. Now cuts in 'dole' (social security payments) and other measures created a distrust of the employer class that still existed in the 1970s. The Depression persuaded the government to abandon Free Trade and go off the Gold Standard – which meant, among other things, that gold coins (not used after 1914) passed permanently out of circulation.

Despite all difficulties, progress was being made. The general direction of wages was upwards, hours of work became shorter, and new industries were developing – electrical and civil engineering, automobiles, chemicals and a whole range of 'service' and 'light' industries.

Recovery from the Second World War was slow, but it was carried out with a determination not to return to pre-war inequalities and unemployment. Two World Wars had made planning and controlling the economy ('war socialism') familiar and this was to be the pattern of the future.

The town of Jarrow was badly hit by unemployment and the reckless march on London in protest in 1936

Shell/Esso oil production platform in the North Sea. Oil has become an important factor in Britain's economy

The Labour Government of 1945–51 nationalised major industries that were flagging (railways, coal mines). It also created a Welfare State intended to protect people against unemployment, sickness and old age, help them through pregnancy and parenthood, and generally to reduce inequalities and social misfortune.

The 1950s and 1960s brought unheard-of prosperity, transforming the lives of ordinary people. Worries about the fundamental soundness of the economy remained, and government involvement and intervention grew steadily greater.

Attempts to forge a national policy controlling wages and prices were unsuccessful, since they failed to satisfy the trade unions, which had become extremely powerful since 1945. But matters only began to seem serious in about 1973. A threat to the oil supplies of the Western world triggered a general economic crisis involving rapidly rising prices (inflation) and high unemployment. Britain was one of the worst-hit Western countries, and this produced a greater degree of co-operation between government, unions and employers. However, living standards remained high, and great hopes were placed in newly discovered reserves of North Sea oil and gas.

In 1973 Britain joined the European Economic Community (or Common Market), a decision that encouraged the adoption of a metric system. The first step was 'decimalisation': shillings disappeared and pennies became $£\frac{1}{100}$ instead of $£\frac{1}{240}$.

Welwyn Garden City, Hertfordshire, was designed and built in the 1920s, to provide an attractive urban centre in the countryside. *Inset:* Darlington factory using modern building materials to create clean cut lines

Buildings

Government intervention began early in the twentieth century with the building of council housing estates to provide low rent accommodation. Housing shortages had already appeared, thanks to population increase and the decay of Victorian housing; all the same, many slums survived until destroyed by Second World War German bombing or post-war clearance schemes. Government ministries

acquired wide powers – including compulsory purchase – in the interests of 'town and country planning', and a man who wanted to build a house had to get permission. Among the more impressive results of this kind of control were the New Towns, skilfully planned communities protected by a 'green belt'; they owed something to the garden city movement.

The main style of twentieth century building has been severe and undecorated. Starkness seemed to go with new materials such as steel, reinforced concrete and glass sheeting. Not only office blocks, but very tall tower blocks for flat-dwellers ('high-rise' housing) are built in this style. It also allows prefabrication – the mass-production of standardised parts – which keeps down costs. High-rise schemes have been popular of recent years because they occupy less valuable ground space than conventional houses, but it is now widely believed that they may have an unhealthy isolating effect on their tenants, and many stand empty and vandalised.

A modern kitchen is a clean, bright place, full of labour-saving devices – cookers, fridges, mixers, electric kettles, toasters, and so on. A hundred years ago things were very different

Interiors & furniture

Mass-produced furnishings improved in design and quality. A vast range of conveniences became steadily more available, and near-universal by the 1960s: electric fires, kettles and irons, central heating, washing machines, refrigerators, vacuum cleaners. Pianos were replaced by radios, and later by television sets and record players. New materials such as plastic, vinyl and synthetic fabrics were lighter and easier to clean. But there were also items that lost their attractiveness when the 'natural' material became too expensive to use. Present-day interest in antiques owes much to the appeal of 'natural' materials and individual manufacture.

All this made housework far less of a burden, especially when shopping was made easier by supermarkets with convenience foods. Above all it made the middle-class style of life possible for millions of people, and without servants – a situation unthinkable in any previous period. In fact this style of family life was partly maintained by the earnings of millions of women who were able to go out to work instead of cooking and cleaning all day.

Clothing & appearance

Men's clothes became even more casual. After the First World War the lounge suit emerged as standard wear, and the 'sports' jacket (not matching the trousers) became acceptable on all but quite formal occasions. Wing and high-stand collars and cravats gave way to soft collars and ties. Most of the paraphernalia of nineteenth century dress tended to disappear or be confined to special occasions – waistcoats, watchchains, hats, gloves, cuff-links and so on.

With more money to spend, young people began to influence fashion from the 1950s e.g. the 'teddy-boy' style. Casualness became even more marked in the

Family fashions of the '20s and '30s

1960s, when older standards of what was 'respectable' disappeared. Denim jeans and jackets established themselves – apparently permanently – as a sort of uniform throughout the Western World, worn by both men and women. Many other styles and trends came and went. One of the most colourful was the 'hippie' look (voluminous 'caftan' robes, headbands, sandals and beads) also worn by both sexes. There were many revivals, such as wide trousers like the 'Oxford bags' of the 1920s, and there was a range of styles to choose from at any one time. The same was true of hair – very long hair appeared in the 1960s, but many different lengths and cuts were acceptable.

Women's fashions were often

1940's

1950's

linked with their growing freedom. The 1920s look was deliberately 'unfeminine' – hipless and breastless, with the waistline marked out round the hips. Skirts were shorter than ever before (knee-length) and hair too was short. The 1930s and 1940s were more conventional, and wartime outfits necessarily sturdy and sensible – officially standardised chunky-looking 'utility' designs, with short skirts to save material. After the war the 'New Look' was deliberately full and 'feminine' in reaction against previous austerity.

Like menswear, women's clothes of recent years have been notable for variety and daring. A few examples are the 'sack', the miniskirt, trouser-suits and 'hot pants' (tight shortest-of-short shorts). The greatest change of all has been the improved quality, design and adventurousness of mass-produced clothes, pioneered by designer Mary Quant and others. Although Paris remained the centre of expensive high fashion, in the 1960s, London became the fashion centre for the young.

A selection of fashions from four decades, starting with the wartime style and the full-skirted post war New Look. This is only a selection, mainly of youth styles, because there were many changes in each period and many differences between age — and other groups

Social system

Hostility between the classes largely disappeared after the First World War, and after the Second, classes themselves became harder to identify. The leisured gentleman became rare; owners were replaced in large concerns by managers of varying importance, and affluence and greater informality wiped out many visible differences between classes. The very concept of the gentleman had virtually disappeared by the 1960s. Class feelings continued to exist, but were increasingly based on differences in income and on the type of work performed.

The basis of class distinction – differences in wealth – remained, though modified by welfare policies, heavier taxation of the better-off. These made it hard to keep together the great estates of the past, and many historic houses passed into the hands of the National Trust. But more fluid forms of wealth were often successfully preserved, and in fact a very high percentage of national wealth remained in the hands of a very small percentage of the population. Education and employment opportunities were also by no means equal, but there is no doubt that these were vastly improved after the Second World War.

Government & justice

The two-party system operated for almost the whole of the period, though the Labour Party replaced the Liberals as the main opponents of Conservatism. Parties became more organised and disciplined, so that MPs had less real independence than in the nineteenth century. Power was increasingly concentrated in the hands of the Cabinet, ruled more or less firmly by the prime minister.

At the same time, government power and responsibility increased enormously. Labour governments nationalised major industries and set up the Welfare State, while the Conservatives remained attached to ideas of 'free enterprise'. But in practice governments of both parties intervened more and more in national life. Ministers and civil servants were granted ever wider powers to make regulations, compulsorily purchase land and houses and so on. By the 1970s many people felt that Britain had become 'over-governed', while others blamed the huge number of 'unproductive' government employees for Britain's economic troubles.

Feelings like this, backed by

national resentments, provided support for the Scottish and Welsh Nationalist movements. These were successful enough to set the leaders of the main parties thinking about devolution – giving some element of self-government to Scotland and Wales. The opposite course was followed in Northern Ireland, which had its own parliament until the troubles of the 1960s and '70s led to its suspension. The province was then ruled directly from Westminster.

Southern Ireland was virtually independent from 1922, though not technically a republic until 1948.

Her political history has been relatively uneventful since the civil war of 1922, in which those who opposed the peace treaty with Britain were finally defeated.

In joining the Common Market, both Britain and Ireland entered into long-term agreements which sacrificed part of their sovereignty. Some people believe they will eventually become provinces of a new United Europe.

During this period there was a growing belief that criminals should be reformed not punished. In the United Kingdom capital punishment was abolished in 1969.

The headquarters of the European Economic Community in Brussels. *Inset:* Roy Jenkins, president of the Community

War & defence

The World Wars influenced British society in a multitude of ways. The Army fought in many parts of the World, the Navy twice beat off the threat of German U-boats (submarines) and a new arm, the Air Force, distinguished itself in the Battle of Britain and the bombing of Germany. Ordinary civilians experienced war at first hand – during enemy bombing raids and as members of the armed services. Conscription (compulsory service) was introduced for all able-bodied men in 1916 and 1939, and women too joined the services or did war work.

A scene from the 'Blitz' — the intensive bombing of British cities in the Second World War. Rescuers clear away rubble in a desperate search for survivors, while a warden helps those who have become homeless

After 1945 Britain joined NATO (North Atlantic Treaty Organisation) and other Western alliances and there was even peacetime conscription (to 1960) at the height of the Cold War. Realising that she could not compete with the 'superpowers' (USA and USSR), Britain gradually reduced her forces, though she manufactured nuclear weapons. In the 1970s the army was used to combat terrorism in Northern Ireland.

The new Irish state remained neutral in the Second World War. From the 1960s its small army was involved in several United Nations 'peacekeeping' operations.

Above: The Central London Mosque, Regent's Park, London

Religion

The Anglican Church in Wales was disestablished in 1919, after long and strong pressure from Welsh Nonconformists.

The striking feature of the age was its indifference to organised religion. Churchgoing declined dramatically, and many churches were closed. Most people apparently continued to believe vaguely in Christianity, or at least in a benevolent God, though nineteenth century habits such as family prayers and Sunday observance were given up. Among highly educated people, disbelief became common, either as agnosticism ('don't-know-ism') or outright atheism (disbelief). Only in the Irish Republic did a church – the Catholic Church – continue to exercise strong popular and political influence.

Their common weakness encouraged the churches to put aside their differences. In 1972 Congregationalists and Presbyterians joined together in a new United Reformed Church. But Anglicans and Methodists narrowly failed to agree, and contacts between Protestants and the Roman Catholic Church remained tentative.

The arrival of Indian and Pakistani immigrants in large numbers meant that Muslims and Hindus now became substantial British religious minorities.

Communications

Most of the fundamental discoveries were made in the nineteenth century. But in the twentieth they were developed tremendously – aeroplanes to jumbo jets and Concordes, motor cars to sleek, efficient mass-produced objects, ships to nuclear-powered submarines and super-tankers. Motor cycles and scooters, helicopters and hovercraft were invented, and 'juggernaut' lorries carried great loads over long distances. Rockets penetrated outer space and satellites orbited the earth, making world-wide communication – and spying – possible.

Transport has developed tremendously in the past fifty years

The social consequences were equally important. With the affluence of the 1950s, air travel and holidays abroad were experienced by many British people and the majority of families were able to buy a motor car.

Two romantic forms of travel were in their heyday between the World Wars: the airship, which proved too disaster-prone, and the luxury ocean-liner, which eventually became too expensive to run.

During those years, radio and films became enormously popular. Most of the films were made in Hollywood, California, and strengthened American influence on British life. Television began in the 1930s, was suspended during the war, and began to be common in the 1950s, again as a result of affluence. Colour transmission followed in 1967. With so much competition, newspapers found it hard to survive; most of those that succeeded became 'tabloids', with large headlines and photographs.

Left: Advertising poster for the American '30s musical, 'Top Hat'. *Right:* In modern primary schools, the value of a creative play — painting and modelling and collecting — is emphasized. Compare this cheerful place with the Victorian schoolroom on page 152

Education

Educational policy in Britain became increasingly a national matter, worked out by the government and applied by local authorities. Down to 1944 it was roughly true to say that upper-class children went to public schools, middle-class children to grammar schools, and working-class children to 'day schools' which they left at fourteen.

From 1944 children in the state system went to two main types of school, the grammar and the secondary modern. They were allocated according to their results in the 'eleven-plus' examination – a system increasingly criticised as making eleven-year-old second-class citizens of those who failed and went to 'secondary mods'. In the 1960s and 1970s there was a long slow change-over to 'comprehensive' education, with a single type of secondary school for all in the state system. The minimum leaving age was raised to fifteen in 1947, and to sixteen in 1972. University students were mainly children of the well-off until the 1950s. But with the adoption of a system of grants to finance study, large numbers of other young people were given their chance. There was an enormous expansion of university and technical education; the old institutions were packed to the limit and many new colleges and universities (for example Sussex University) were founded. A fascinating new experiment, the Open University, began in 1971. It offered degree courses based on correspondence teaching, radio and television broadcasts, local group activity and summer schools.

Art & ornament

In the twentieth century Britain produced some distinguished artists, but most of them worked in the great modern styles pioneered abroad – cubism, abstractionism,

York University

expressionism, pop art and so on. However, at least one British artist, the sculptor Henry Moore, was generally accepted as a world master.

Individual craftsmen survived, and from the 1950s affluence created a greater demand for their work. But more important for the general

A Henry Moore sculpture

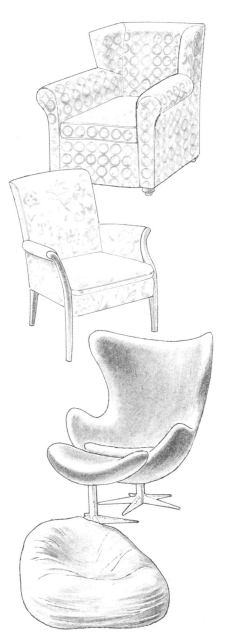

quality of life was the improved design of factory-made goods. It first became apparent in the 1920s, when a wide range of smaller, generally more expensive items were made in the geometrical Art Deco style. By the 1960s even the humblest household goods were being made with pleasingly clean and simple shapes and patterns.

Designs for modern chairs. Traditional designs remain popular, as the top two examples show. But in the last few years many people have preferred modernistic designs to enclose and support the body, or the 'sag-bag' casual seat that moulds itself to your shape

Leisure

Radios and films transformed entertainment after the First World War. From about 1930 all films were 'talkies'. The cinema's popularity declined sharply from the 1950s, with the introduction and gradual improvement of television, which became the dominant entertainment medium.

Sports developed into great popular spectacles, watched by millions of people, run for profit, and starring highly paid professionals. Even traditionally amateur games such as tennis became professionalised. Football became the national sport.

More and more money was spent on gambling, especially after the law was relaxed in 1960. Horse

racing, football pools and bingo were the most popular forms.

Popular music gained a new importance with Rock and Roll in the 1950s; the new 'pop' became part of the way of life of young people rather than just entertainment. The Beatles and other groups were worshipped as film stars had previously been. Stereo record players, long-playing records and mass open-air pop festivals all gave added force to the trend.

Music-making in the home became less common with radio, hi-fi and so on. Paradoxically, Britain now produced her first great composers since Purcell (Benjamin Britten, Michael Tippett).

Post-war affluence and special cheap 'package' arrangements made foreign travel possible for millions.

History on view

A great many items mentioned in this chapter, from council housing to decimal coinage, hardly need identifying. The World Wars have left their marks too – notably the memorials in every town and village. Lists of Second World War dead have simply been added to the First World War memorials (an interesting economic measure), and a comparative count demonstrates how much more punishing trench warfare was. Pill-boxes on the Cumbrian coast date from the days when a German invasion seemed likely. And the few surviving 'pre-fabs' – dingy, flat-roofed concrete bungalows – are what remains of the scheme that provided instant housing for people who had been 'bombed out'. London's **Imperial War Museum** presents the military record.

Some of the more ambitious examples of modern British architecture are **Liverpool** and **Coventry Cathedrals**, and the **South Bank Arts Complex** and the **Barbican** development in London.

White Tower, Tower of London

There are many, many interesting places I have not named, mainly through lack of space. But there are also some others that should really have been mentioned in every

Windsor Castle, Berkshire

single chapter – for example, the great national art collections in London, Edinburgh and Dublin. Instead of such repetition, here is a

Queen Elizabeth Hall on London's South Bank

list of a few such places:

Many periods of history are covered by the **National Portrait Gallery** in Trafalgar Square, the **Tower of London**, and **Windsor Castle**. Two lesser-known museums have series of life-size model interiors from various periods: the **Geffrye Museum**, London, and

National Maritime Museum, Greenwich, London

Victorian Room at Geffrye Museum, London

the **Castle Museum**, York. The finest collection of sixteenth to twentieth century clothing, often shown in their contemporary settings, is at the **Bath Museum of Costume.**

Early post office at Castle Museum, York

The National Army Museum, Chelsea, covers the whole period down to 1914, after which the Imperial War Museum takes over. For the navy there is the **National Maritime Museum**, Greenwich; for the air force the **RAF Museum**, Hendon.

The **Victoria and Albert Museum** and the **London Museum** have a little of everything, and of course there are local museums all over the British Isles, almost all of them with at least a few really worthwhile items. Finally, a huge number of buildings have been remodelled and added to over the centuries: castles, cathedrals, churches, most of the great houses open to the public. They and their contents represent living history – an accumulation that can, however, seem like an impossibly confusing jumble. One of the main aims of this book is to help you make sense of it all.

Time Chart

British Isles	World

Roman Britain

BC

55
54 Caesar's expeditions to Britain

44 Caesar's assassination
AD

43 Conquest of Britain
61 Revolt led by Boudicca
122–126 Building of Hadrian's Wall

330 Constantinople founded
410 Visigoths sack Rome

Saxons, Scots and Vikings

c. 432 St Patrick begins
conversion of Ireland

476 End of Roman Empire
in the West

597 St Augustine arrives in Kent

634 Arabs begin conquest of Middle
East and North Africa
663 Synod of Whitby

800 Charlemagne crowned
Holy Roman Emperor
843 Picts and Scots united
1016–42 England ruled by
Danish kings
1066 Battle of Hastings
Norman conquest

Feudal Britain

1086 Domesday survey

1094 First crusade
1187 Saladin recaptures Jerusalem
from Crusaders
1215 Magna Carta sealed at
Runnymede
1241 Mongols invade Europe
1283 English conquer Wales
1314 Scots defeat English
at Bannockburn

The Later Middle Ages

1338–1453 Hundred Years War
1348 The Black Death

1378 The Great Schism
(rival popes)
1431 Joan of Arc burned

British Isles	World
1453 Loss of English possessions in France (except Calais) **1455** First battles of the Wars of the Roses **1485** Richard III defeated and killed at the battle of Bosworth. End of the Wars of the Roses. Henry VII first Tudor king.	**1453** Turks capture Constantinople **1480** Muscovy (later Russia) becomes independent of Mongols **1486** Diaz, Portuguese navigator, rounds Cape of Good Hope

Renaissance and Reformation

1529 English Reformation begins **1560** Triumph of Protestantism in Scotland **1588** Spanish Armada	**1492** Columbus reaches America **1517** Martin Luther makes protest which starts Reformation **1529** Turks besiege Vienna **1539** Jesuits (Society of Jesus) founded **1567** Revolt of the Netherlands against Spanish rule

The Seventeenth Century

1603 Death of Queen Elizabeth I. James I and VI: union of English/Scottish crowns **1642–46** English Civil War **1649** Charles I executed: Commonwealth (republic) until 1660 **1653–58** Oliver Cromwell Lord Protector **1660** Charles II restored to throne **1688** 'Glorious Revolution' James II deposed	**1618–48** Thirty Years War in central Europe **1620** *Mayflower* sails to America **1638** Japan closed to Europeans **1689–1713** European Wars. Britain and others in alliance against France

The Eighteenth Century

1707 Political union between England and Scotland **1745** Jacobite rebellion	**1756–63** Seven Years War **1776** American Declaration of Independence

British Isles	World
	1789 Start of the French
1801 British/Irish union	Revolution
1807 Abolition of slave trade	
in British Empire	**1812** Napoleon's retreat from
1815 Battle of Waterloo.	Moscow
End of Napoleonic wars	

Age of Industrial Revolution

1819 'Peterloo' massacre of
reform demonstrators
1832 Great Reform Bill
1841–46 Britain becomes Free
Trade country
1846 Irish famine

                              1848 Year of European revolutions

1854–56 Crimean War

                              1861–65 US Civil War
                              1870–71 Franco-Prussian War
                              German Empire founded
                              1903 First aeroplane flight by
                              Wright brothers

1909 First Old Age Pensions
1914–18   The First World War

Modern Times

1916 Easter rebellion in Ireland

                              1917 Russian Revolution

1918/1928 British women given vote
1922 Irish Free State set up
1926 General Strike
1929–33   Wall Street Collapse: Great Depression
                         1933 Hitler comes to power in Germany
                         1936–39 Spanish Civil War
1939–45   The Second World War
1945–51 Labour Government:
         'Austerity', nationalisation,
         Welfare State
1949 Ireland becomes republic   **1949** China becomes communist state
                         1950–53 Korean War
                         1963 President Kennedy assassinated
                         1969 Apollo 11: first men on moon

1973 Britain and Ireland join
Common Market

                         1975 Communist victory in Vietnam

Index